American Race Relations and the Legacy of British Colonialism

Colonial rule distorts a colony's economy and its society, and British rule was no exception. British policies led to a stratified American colonial society with slaves on the bottom and white settlers on top. The divided society functioned through laws that imposed rules and defined roles of the respective races. This occurred in other colonies, too, often leading to strife that continues today. Especially since World War II, the United States seems finally to have been able to remove many laws and practices that had created barriers between races in the divided society. Appeals to legitimacy, such as by abolitionists and the Civil Rights Movement, were essential to change laws from support of the divided society to instruments for disestablishing it. Thanks to the rule of law – another important British legacy – the U.S. is much farther along than many former colonies in making progress. By highlighting the history of the interplay of two fundamental concepts, the divided society and the rule of law, and briefly contrasting the experiences of other former colonies, this book shows how the United States has made significant long-term progress, although incomplete, and ways for this to continue today.

Thomas H. Stanton is a Fellow of the National Academy of Public Administration, and teaches as an adjunct faculty member at the Center for Advanced Governmental Studies at Johns Hopkins University. Website: www.thomas-stanton.com.

American Race Relations and the Legacy of British Colonialism

Thomas H. Stanton

LONDON AND NEW YORK

First published 2020 by Routledge

2 Park Square, Milton Park, Abingdon, Oxon OX14 4RN
605 Third Avenue, New York, NY 10017

Routledge is an imprint of the Taylor & Francis Group, an informa business

First issud in paperback 2021

Publisher's Note

The publisher has gone to great lengths to ensure the quality of this reprint but points out that some imperfections in the original copies may be apparent.

Library of Congress Cataloging-in-Publication Data
Names: Stanton, Thomas H., 1944– author.
Title: American race relations and the legacy of British colonialism / Thomas H. Stanton.
Description: New York, NY : Routledge/Taylor & Francis Group, 2020. | Includes bibliographical references and index.
Identifiers: LCCN 2019059940 (print) | LCCN 2019059941 (ebook) | ISBN 9780367423216 (hardback) | ISBN 9780367823504 (ebook) | ISBN 9781000053098 (adobe pdf) | ISBN 9781000053104 (mobi) | ISBN 9781000053111 (epub)
Subjects: LCSH: African Americans—Legal status, laws, etc.—United States—History. | Slavery—Law and legislation—United States—History. | United States—Race relations—History. | United States—Colonial influence.
Classification: LCC E185 .S794 2020 (print) | LCC E185 (ebook) | DDC 305.800973—dc23
LC record available at https://lccn.loc.gov/2019059940
LC ebook record available at https://lccn.loc.gov/2019059941

ISBN: 978-0-367-42321-6 (hbk)
ISBN: 978-1-03-217395-5 (pbk)
DOI: 10.4324/9780367823504

Typeset in Times New Roman
by Apex CoVantage, LLC

To my wife, Martha Zaslow,
who is my best friend

Contents

	Acknowledgments	viii
1	Introduction and Overview	1
2	Colonial Economies, Societies, and Laws	4
3	The Rule of Law and Its Significance	16
4	Law and America's Divided Society	35
5	Conclusion: Overcoming the Colonial History of America's Divided Society	61
	Index	64

Acknowledgments

The author wishes to thank the many people who reviewed the manuscript and made valuable comments.

1 Introduction and Overview

Colonial rule is different from other forms of government. That's because the ruling country has goals and purposes that differ from those of the local people, and the capacity to impose its will. Colonial rule distorts both a colony's economy and its society, and British rule was no exception. In its pursuit of economic gain, Britain created distortions in America's society with effects that continue even today. Most importantly, British policies led to the importation of slave labor, which provided generous economic returns from the sale of enslaved people, from related enterprises such as the shipping industry, and especially from the sale of the agricultural products that slaves produced. This economic drive had social consequences in creating a stratified American colonial society with slaves on the bottom and white settlers on top. Effects of British colonialism include not only creation of such a society but also continuing British shaping of the American South to be a virtual colonial agricultural economy, both before and after the Civil War.

Even while creating a divided colonial society, British rule also gave to the United States the "rule of law," which is a major source of strength as the United States has sought to overcome the legacy of that divided society. The rule of law, despite its apparently simple meaning, involves complexities and sometimes contradictory meanings that people and governments might impute to the idea. This book adopts a specific concept of the rule of law, based on a government that has limited its own authority to engage in arbitrary actions vis-à-vis its subjects and that is governed by a legal system that those subject to the law have a hand in shaping. The rule of law inclines people to obey laws because they believe that the legal system is legitimate, rather than merely because they fear adverse consequences if they disobey.

A fundamental division in American society, based on slavery and laws that maintained slavery, lasted from colonial times to the Civil War. To hold the 13 colonies together, the framers of the U.S. Constitution made compromises to accommodate slavery and states' rights and to provide disproportionate electoral strength for southern slave states. For whites, the Constitution guaranteed the rule of law, while black slaves remained subject to an authoritarian "rule by law." Without sufficient possibilities to resolve these issues within the political or legal systems, a civil war occurred before the U.S. formally abolished slavery.

Even after the Civil War, southern states used the law as an instrument to maintain economic benefits of compulsory servitude of former slaves while nominally granting them freedom. Again, rule by law, this time over emancipated slaves, played a major role in sustaining a divided society. Even though Congress forced the addition of new Civil Rights Amendments to the Constitution after the Civil War, state laws and decisions of the U.S. Supreme Court eliminated much of their benefit.

A fundamentally divided American society persisted until well into the twentieth century. Even in the New Deal, programs favored whites over blacks in both design and implementation. Finally, World War II brought a turning point in the attack on the divided society in the United States. As public sensitivity to civil rights grew, courts and the national government more generally became active in addressing race discrimination. The rule of law came into play as the key instrument for deconstructing the divided society in America. In contrast to other colonies and their divided societies, the fact that the United States had a rule of law meant that social division could be addressed by including people of all races in those whom the rule of law benefited. This was a difficult task, but one that was easier than trying first to adopt the rule of law and then using it to address the problem of social division.

The effort at overcoming the colonial history of a divided society is succeeding in the United States, although only after many years and a Civil War, to an extent that has not been possible in post-colonial societies that lack institutions and cultures based on strong support for the rule of law. While the United States has achieved notable success, the legacy of a stratified colonial beginning has left considerable work undone. Under the rule of law, the content of particular laws, court decisions, and implementation of laws changes back and forth in response to prevailing political and cultural views. Sometimes political winds shift to encourage favorable laws in the effort to reduce social divisions, and sometimes there are adverse changes. Yet, the rule of law built into the American constitutional system means that adverse changes are limited in the extent that they can quickly move society backwards again. This book reviews the arc of history and variations in the American legal system over time to show the substantial, although incomplete, progress that the United States has made toward ending the divided society that is a legacy of British colonialism.

2 Colonial Economies, Societies, and Laws

Defenders of the British Empire point to its positive benefits, including global trade and capital markets, the spread of rule of law and civil administration, and the ubiquity of the English language (Ferguson, 2002, pp. 358–364). Yet, the other side of the ledger cannot be ignored. It was British colonialism that created the challenges of black-white race relations in the United States today, to say nothing of its contribution to the racial, ethnic, and religious strife that continues to bedevil former British colonies around the globe. While each colony's experience was different, the pattern of British rule created similarities in other countries that shed light on the American experience as well.

Economic Drivers of British Colonialism and American Slavery

Colonial conquest was driven largely by the pursuit of economic gain. English interaction with the New World began in the sixteenth century. Seafarers undertook voyages of discovery and foreign trade and privateer ventures against the Spanish. Early voyages were funded individually by investors; when a ship returned with cargo and profits, the owners divided the proceeds and then funded another expedition.

As the volume of trade increased, merchants developed the concept of the joint-stock company: rather than investing in the proceeds of an individual voyage, investors purchased stock in a company chartered by the Crown to engage in trade within specifically demarcated boundaries. Often, as an incentive for investors, the Crown would authorize chartered companies to hold a monopoly over their authorized domains. In return the Crown would receive a share of the proceeds. Thus were born the great royal companies, including the Russia Company, the English East India Company, the Hudson's Bay Company, and – most unfortunately – the Royal African Company (Brock, 1887).

Other companies relevant to the New World included the Massachusetts Bay Company, the Virginia Company, and other companies authorized to establish plantations and to colonize particular parts of North America (Tomlins, 2001, p. 343). Establishment of white settlements was a means to achieve economic ends and to help exploit America's abundant natural resources (Beer, 1922, pp. 53–77). Thus, the 13 colonies became settler colonies, similar to Ireland, Canada, South Africa, Rhodesia (now Zimbabwe), Australia, and New Zealand, which involved large numbers of British and other European settlers who sought to dominate or displace indigenous peoples (Huttenback, 1976). Settler colonies stood in contrast to the many British colonies, such as India or the Caribbean colonies, that were governed and controlled by a small minority of British administrators.

In the nineteenth century Britain enacted Companies Acts, allowing investors to establish companies without regard to limitations specified in a royal charter. This helped to promote competition that might have been constrained by the language of specialized company charters issued earlier. The progression of organizational forms, together with advances in shipping technology, increased the scale available to English adventurers and ship owners to engage in the transportation of not only colonists but also indentured laborers and slaves and the agricultural products they produced.

Besides offering a haven for those colonists seeking better lives, colonization of North America also served a variety of purposes for the Crown, and especially economic purposes. Historian George Louis Beer observed that some

> favored colonization as a remedy for overpopulation and social distress; but far more emphasis was laid on colonization as a means of quickening English commerce and of freeing England from what, according to prevailing economic theories, was a dangerous dependence on rival nations . . . the colony was to be primarily a source of supply for the metropolis.
>
> (1922, pp. 53, 66)

It was no accident that the Board of Trade and its precursors played a major role in British administration of the 13 American colonies (Beer, 1922, pp. 337–338).

Operating under a mercantilist philosophy, British policymakers saw colonization as a means to provide raw materials and help to reduce British dependence on foreign sources of supply. In addition to providing imports to Britain itself, products of the 13 American colonies, especially tobacco, brought Britain considerable revenue when shipped to Western Europe (Price, 1998). Investors in royal companies, and later in commerce more generally, sought their own economic returns.

This approach placed the American colonies in a position of economic subordination, and British efforts to strengthen the home country's position vis-à-vis the colonies aroused American ire. Thus, the tea that merchants and their compatriots threw into Boston Harbor during the Tea Party in 1773 belonged to the East India Company, which operated under British law as a monopoly that the Americans considered threatening to their livelihoods (Schlesinger, 1918). Many of the grievances listed in the Declaration of Independence related to the customs service that Britain used to enforce the Navigation Acts and other economic requirements that Britain sought to impose:

> An American reading of that passage in the Declaration of Independence which denounces the king because he had "erected a multitude of New Offices, and sent hither swarms of Officers to harass our people, and eat out their substance" would understand this reference to the customs officials. More specifically, the complaints in the Declaration that the colonists had been deprived "in many cases, of the benefits of Trial by Jury" and transported "beyond Seas to be tried for pretend offices" singled out the Admiralty court system which was a major element in the customs apparatus.
>
> (Barrow, 1967, p. 256)

In addition, Barrow notes, a major complaint in the Declaration against the king was "For cutting off our Trade with all parts of the world."

Along with profitability to the home country, British colonial rule emphasized an unwillingness to pay much for colonial administration. Jack Greene (1994, p. 15) notes how the reluctance of Britain to pay for large overseas military and civil establishments shifted considerable governance and power from the home country to the colonies. When the British parliament sought to assert greater control and to impose new trade rules and taxes on the colonies, the result was a crisis that exposed the growing differences between a home country that believed it possessed the right to rule and American colonists who believed that they had the rights of Englishmen to influence the process of making laws that they would be required to obey.

Profits also drove the slave trade. As Niall Ferguson (2002, pp. 78–79) puts it, "slavery made overwhelming sense as an economic proposition." William Robert Scott (1912, reprinted 1968), in his classic treatise on English, Scottish, and Irish joint-stock companies, writes of the origins of the English slave trade in 1562:

> The commencement of the English slave trade was no after-thought but the original foundation of the venture, since [John] Hawkins formulated his scheme on the basis of negroes being "very good merchandise in Hispaniola." During the cruise off the coast of Africa 300 slaves were obtained "partly by the sword, partly by other means." Sales were made in the West Indies on such a profitable scale that Hawkins was able not only to fully load his three ships with hides, ginger and sugar, besides some pearls, but in addition he had to procure two other ships to carry the overplus.
>
> (Scott, Vol. II, p. 8)

The English slave trade grew from there. Slavery in the southern North American colonies began slowly after 1619 and gained momentum by the mid-1700s (Beer, 1922, p. 266). While precise numbers are lacking, one estimate is that from 1601 to 1867, a total of 361,000 slaves were transported to British North America (Eltis, 2001, Table III, Volume of Transatlantic Slave Arrivals by Region of Arrival [in thousands]).

At first, southern planters deployed slaves to grow tobacco, rice, and indigo. Then, as friction with Britain turned into open hostilities and the Revolutionary War, planters turned to producing cotton goods to substitute for textile imports that in peacetime had come from Britain. In the 1790s demand for cotton increased, and the invention of the cotton gin helped to make cotton more profitable. The slave population imported to South Carolina and Georgia to grow cotton dramatically increased and continued to grow (Beckert, 2015, pp. 101–103; Chapin, 1991). By 1860 the U.S. Census recorded 3,953,750 slaves present in the United States (U.S. Census Bureau, 1860).

While the favorable climate for cotton and other agricultural products confined slavery largely to the South, merchants in the North became heavily involved in both the slave trade and the export of slave-grown products from the South to Britain and elsewhere in the world. With respect to the slave trade itself, a sophisticated retrospective analysis conducted at Brown University reports, for instance, that "Rhode Islanders dominated the North American share of the African slave trade, mounting over a thousand slaving voyages in the century before the abolition of the trade in 1807 (and scores more illegal voyages thereafter)" (Brown University Steering Committee on Slavery and Justice, 2006, October, p. 3).[1] Northern shippers also profited from transporting cotton, which, in 1860, amounted to almost 60 percent of the value of all U.S. merchandise exports, and had been produced largely by slaves (Beckert, 2015, pp. 205–206). For those who benefited, slavery was very profitable.

Once British manufacturing became stronger and Britain became a low-cost producer of many manufactured products, mercantilism gave way to a philosophy of free trade under which Britain would expect to prevail in economic competition with rivals. Eventually, it also became clear to British leaders that informal control and economic influence (i.e., de facto colonialism) could be more advantageous than actual colonial settlement:

> The types of informal empire and the situations it attempted to exploit were as various as the success which it achieved. . . . In the United States, for example, British business turned the cotton South into a colonial economy, and the British investor hoped to do the same with the Mid-West. But the political strength of the country stood in his way. It was impossible to stop American industrialization, and the industrialized sections successfully campaigned for tariffs, despite the opposition of those sections which depended on the British trade connexion.
>
> (Gallagher & Robinson, 1953, p. 10)

In other words, the British came to understand that economic control, through what later generations might call neocolonialism, was sufficent to provide desired economic benefits without entailing the burdens of ruling a colony (Robinson & Gallagher, 1967, pp. 4–7). One major consequence was to continue to make slavery profitable for planters and associated stakeholders in the American South even after the British had abolished slavery for themselves.

Besides distorting colonial economies to serve the home country, British rule also distorted colonial societies. Even after colonial rule ended, the benefits to elites and key stakeholders in both Britain and the United States from slavery and the associated agricultural production posed major political obstacles to the difficult task of ending the divided American society that colonialism had helped to establish.

Colonial and Post-Colonial Divided Societies

Driven by economic incentives, colonial rule frequently involved the transplantation of populations to colonies where the imported people could enhance economic returns to the colonial ruler. This distorted colonial social structures, with whites on top and one or more racial groups below. The experience of other British colonies with their continuing divided societies helps in understanding developments in the 13 American colonies afterwards.

British colonial officer and student of the colonial and post-colonial experience J. S. Furnivall (b. 1878–d. 1960) served in Burma for many years both before and after independence. His book *Colonial Policy and Practice* introduced the idea of what he called a "plural society":

> In Burma, as in Java, the first thing that strikes the visitor is the medly of peoples [who] mix but do not combine. Each group holds by its own religion, its own culture and language, its own ideas and ways. As individuals they meet, but only in the market-place, in buying and selling. There is a plural society, with different sections of the community living side-by-side, but separately, within the same political unit. Even in the economic sphere there is a division of labor along racial lines.
>
> (Furnivall, 1956, p. 304)

With only slight adaptations, Furnivall's plural society (what this book also calls a "divided society") helps to highlight important aspects of African slavery in British colonies: the British Empire brought together white and black people, sometimes supplemented by other ethnic groups such as South Asians in Caribbean colonies or East Africa (e.g., Tinker, 1974; Morris, 1956), to obtain valuable cash crops such as sugar cane, rice, indigo, and cotton in service to the imperial economy. People lived in the same colony, stratified into a hierarchical society.

Furnivall's construct should not be confused with terms such as "pluralism" that can apply to more integrated societies than those structured by British colonial rule. Furnivall's plural society is the opposite of the American conception of a "melting pot" or even the Canadian conception of a "mosaic" of different groups living together in the same country: in Furnivall's plural society people from different social groups may inhabit the same location for years without considering themselves to be part of the same society.

As a colonial officer, Furnivall saw that a colonial power such as Britain would provide the essential force to hold different groups together for a common economic purpose. Given the strong economic motive for colonization, it is unsurprising that colonial rule created and greatly strengthened economic forces that caused and sustained the plural society, not only in the 13 American colonies but also in other colonies across the globe. In its most extreme form, colonization released economic forces that tore communities apart and atomized them into economically motivated individuals. This happened in Burma, the colony with which Furnivall was most familiar, where peasants left traditional subsistence agriculture and migrated to areas where they grew rice commercially, participated in the monetized economy, and took on excessive debt (Stanton, 2014; Taylor, 1995).

In Furnivall's plural society, the different groups lack a common political consensus or vision that can help to mitigate the effects of a purely economic purpose because "in a plural society, that is almost all they have in common. Everywhere, in all forms of society, the working of economic forces makes for tension between groups with competing or conflicting interests. . . . In a homogeneous society the tension is alleviated by their common citizenship, but in a plural society there is a corresponding cleavage along racial lines" (Furnivall, 1956, p. 311).

What that meant for a colony was that racial groups, such as whites and blacks in the 13 American colonies, would "coexist spatially, in the same economy, and under the same polity, yet their members have very few crosscutting relationships in a minimal number of settings. There is little true reciprocity and sharing of values" (Holden, 1996, p. 212). In his description of race relations in America before the Civil War, Alexis de Tocqueville put his finger on the critical aspect of the plural society in the United States: whites and blacks coexisted but remained separate. He wrote that this created difficulty for the United States: "the destiny of the Negroes is in some measure interwoven with that of the Europeans. These two races are fastened to each other without intermingling; and they are alike unable to separate entirely or to combine" (de Tocqueville, 1835, Chapter XVIII).

British colonial authorities recognized the lack of a common political and social vision among participants in the plural societies that they governed. Their frequent solution was to rely on autocratic rule rather than allowing for representation by colonial populations. Eric Williams, the first Prime Minister of post-colonial Trinidad and Tobago, described the reaction of the British government to proposals from planters in 1810 that the colony of Trinidad be granted free representation in the House of Assembly and trial by jury. The British government rejected this petition on grounds that the small number of whites would seek to dominate the much larger number of freed slaves on the island and that they also would be likely to oppose implementation of the recent British policy of abolishing the slave trade. Instead, Trinidad became the first official Crown Colony (Williams, 1942), ruled by a British colonial governor and subject to control of the Colonial Office.

The British government came to use a similar argument to justify its imposition of imperial rule across the empire. The spread of colonialism and imperialism often exacerbated local ethnic and religious divisions, and the Crown then could position itself as essential to maintain peace. In India, for example, the British government justified colonial rule by a

> discourse that denied India the status of a nation and portrayed it as a divided society at war with itself. Torn by internal conflict, India was in desperate need, it was claimed, of a neutral and therefore preferably foreign power to govern it and secure the peace. The colonial hope was that the fragmentation of Indian society into innumerable minorities would [make] the British presence seem permanently indispensable.
>
> (Mukherjee, 2010a, p. 466)

For colonies with plural societies and economies based on plural societies, the question eventually became what would happen when the iron hand of British rule was withdrawn. In many cases, the answer was not pretty. Upon gaining independence after World War II, some ex-colonies sought to deal with their plural societies by expelling imported minorities or otherwise pressuring them to leave (e.g., Balachandran,

1981). Soon after its independence, Burma, now Myanmar, expelled hundreds of thousands of South Asians and Chinese. Seven hundred thousand Rohingya, expelled from Myanmar in 2017 (Beech, 2018, February 15), include many descendants of Bengalis whom the British had encouraged to migrate to Burma in the 1820s to cultivate rice (Chan, 2005). Countries such as Malaysia (formerly British Malaya), Sri Lanka (formerly the colony of Ceylon), former British colonies in the Caribbean, and even the Pacific island of Fiji continue to show deep social scars from the importation of South Asian laborers to generate colonial profits and build or deepen plural societies.[2]

Furnivall's contributions to understanding the effects of European colonialism in creating plural societies across the globe continue to be recognized, especially as tensions roil former colonies. In 2014 *The Economist* published a report detailing numerous examples of ethnic tension from Myanmar, Malaysia, and Indonesia (a former Dutch colony), noting that "These events may appear disparate, but they reflect a common thread running through the history of race and religion in South-East Asia. Specifically, they reflect the legacy of those colonial territories which one British academic and colonial administrator, John Furnivall, first characterised as 'plural societies.'"

In the United States, distinctions among races in the plural society were most pronounced with respect to white-black race relations. Other examples of systematic race-based discrimination, such as relations of whites with Asian laborers imported into the western U.S. in the nineteenth and twentieth centuries, while exhibiting white efforts at domination and other attributes of a plural society, are not addressed in the present book (see, e.g., Barth, 1964; Chuman, 1976). This book also omits discussing the tragedy of white relations with Native Americans; settlers dominated Native Americans to take their land more than to exploit their labor and include them in the American plural society.[3]

The core problem of plural societies is that they consist of racial and ethnic groups who were thrown together in the colonial enterprise and who find little in common with each other, even as they compete for resources. Colonialism could be a cruel game: it pitted different ethnic groups and races against one another in a way that exacerbated conflict when the colonial ruler departed, leaving the different parts of a plural society to work out their differences by themselves. Once the British withdrew from a colony and took the lid off the plural society pressure cooker, the result often was a struggle for economic and political dominance by the most powerful group. Deep-seated issues of race, culture, and often religion, as well as communal fears for physical security, have compounded the post-colonial struggle in many countries (e.g., Halliday, Karpik, & Feeley, 2012).

Furnivall's plural society highlights a pattern that helps to explain the lack of political cohesion of many post-colonial societies. Sociologist M. G. Smith views Furnivall's construct as a part of the effort towards building "a conceptual framework appropriate for the systematic comparative study of those historical and contemporary societies whose organization and composition positively blocked their functional or normative integration and minimized their internal cohesion" (Smith, 1971, p. 419).

Colonial rule greatly limited indigenous politics. With exceptions from time to time as strife erupted, the overt social impact of racial and ethnic differences thus would be muted. While there might be inter-group cooperation to throw out a colonial power, that cooperation tended to wane after the colony achieved independence. The results could be loss of life, as in the bloodshed during the partition of India, or imposition of post-colonial authoritarian rule in the name of containing ethnic conflict (Taylor, 1995; Rajah, 2012).

Notes

1. See also Higginbotham (1978), "The Massachusetts colonists viewed the slave trade as their English counterparts did – merely as another form of commercial activity" (p. 63); see also Bailey (1990).
2. On the importation of Indian labor to British colonies, see, e.g., Tinker (1974); Ghee (1984); and Jayawardena and Kurian (2015).
3. The Supreme Court asserted in the mid-nineteenth century, "The native tribes who were found on this continent at the time of its discovery have never been acknowledged or treated as independent nations by the European governments, nor regarded as the owners of the territories they respectively occupied. On the contrary, the whole continent was divided and parceled out, and granted by the governments of Europe as if it had been vacant and unoccupied land, and the Indians continually held to be, and treated as, subject to their dominion and control." Decision by Chief Justice Roger Taney. *United States v. Rogers*, 1846.

Sources Cited

Bailey, R. (1990). The slave(ry) trade and the development of capitalism in the United States: The textile industry in New England. *Social Science History, 14*(3), 373–414.

Balachandran, P. K. (1981). An embattled community: Asians in east Africa today. *African Affairs, 80*(320), 317–325.

Barrow, T. C. (1967). *Trade and empire: The British customs service in colonial America, 1660–1775*. Cambridge, MA: Harvard University Press.

Barth, G. (1964). *Bitter strength: A history of the Chinese in the United States, 1850–1870*. Cambridge, MA: Harvard University Press.

Beckert, S. (2015). *Empire of cotton: A global history*. New York, NY: Alfred A. Knopf.

Beech, H. (2018, February 15). Will the Rohingya ever return home? *New York Times*.

Beer, G. L. (1922). *The origins of the British colonial system, 1578–1660*. New York, NY: Macmillan.

Brock, R. A. (1887). *The fourth charter of the Royal African company of England, September 27, 1672, with prefatory note exhibiting the past relation of Virginia to African slavery*. Richmond, VA: Virginia Historical Society.

Brown University Steering Committee on Slavery and Justice. (2006, October). Slavery and justice. Retrieved from http://brown.edu/Research/Slavery_Justice/documents/SlaveryAndJustice.pdf

Chan, A. (2005). The development of a Muslim enclave in Arakan (Rakhine) state of Burma (Myanmar). *SOAS Bulletin of Burma Research, 3*(2), 396–420.

Chapin, J. E. (1991). Creating a cotton south in Georgia and South Carolina, 1760–1815. *The Journal of Southern History, 57*(2), 171–200.

Chuman, F. F. (1976). *The bamboo people: The law and Japanese Americans*. Del Mar, CA: Publisher's Inc.

de Tocqueville, A. (1835). *Democracy in America*. University Park, PA: Pennsylvania State University, Electronic Classics Series.

Eltis, D. (2001). The volume and structure of the transatlantic slave trade: A reassessment. *The William and Mary Quarterly, 58*(1), 17–46.

Ferguson, N. (2002). *Empire: The rise and demise of the British world order and the lessons for global power*. New York, NY: Basic Books.

Furnivall, J. S. (1956). *Colonial policy and practice: A comparative study of Burma and Netherlands India*. New York, NY: New York University Press.

Gallagher, J., & Robinson, R. (1953). The imperialism of free trade. *The Economic History Review, 6*(1), 1–15.

Ghee, L. T. (1984). British colonial administration and the "ethnic division of labour" in Malaya. *Kajian Malaysia* II, 2, Dis, 28–66.

Greene, J. P. (1994). *Negotiated authorities: Essays in colonial political and constitutional history*. Charlottesville, VA: Virginia University Press.

Halliday, T. C., Karpik, L., & Feeley, M. M. (2012). *Fates of political liberalism in the British post-colony: The politics of the legal complex*. New Delhi: Cambridge University Press.

Higginbotham, A. L., Jr. (1978). *In the matter of color: Race and the American legal process, the colonial period*. New York, NY: Oxford University Press.

Holden, M., Jr. (1996). *Public administration and the plural society continuity and disruption: Essays in public administration*. Pittsburgh, PA: University of Pittsburgh Press.

Huttenback, R. A. (1976). *Racism and empire: White settlers and colored immigrants in the British self-governing colonies, 1830–1910*. Ithaca, NY: Cornell University Press.

Jayawardena, K., & Kurian, R. (2015). *Class, patriarchy and ethnicity on Sri Lankan plantations: Two centuries of power and protest*. New Delhi: Orient Blackswan Private Limited.

Morris, S. (1956). Indians in East Africa: A study in a plural society. *The British Journal of Sociology*, *7*(3), 194–211.

Mukherjee, M. (2010a). Transcending Identity: Gandhi, nonviolence, and the pursuit of a "different" freedom in modern India. *The American Historical Review*, *115*(2), 453–473.

Price, J. M. (1998). The imperial economy, 1700–1776. In *The Oxford history of the British empire: Vol. II: The eighteenth century* (pp. 78–104). Oxford: Oxford University Press.

Rajah, J. (2012). *Authoritarian rule of law: Legislation, discourse, and legitimacy in Singapore*. Cambridge: Cambridge University Press.

Robinson, R., & Gallagher, J., with Denny, A (1967). *Africa and the Victorians: The official mind of imperialism*. London: Macmillan.

Schlesinger, A. M. (1918). *The colonial merchants and the American Revolution*. New York, NY: Columbia University Press.

Scott, W. R. (1912, reprinted 1968). *The constitution and finance of English, Scottish and Irish joint stock companies to 1720* (Vol. II). Cambridge: Cambridge University Press.

Smith, M. G. (1971). Some developments in the analytic framework of pluralism. In L. Kuper & M. G. Smith (Eds.), *Pluralism in Africa* (pp. 415–458). Berkeley, CA: University of California Press.

Stanton, T. H. (2014). Law and economic development: The cautionary tale of colonial Burma. *Asian Journal of Law and Society*, *1*(1), 1–17.

Taylor, R. H. (1995). Disaster or release? J. S. Furnivall and the bankruptcy of Burma. *Modern Asian Studies*, *44*(1), 45–63.

The Economist (US). (2014, August 2). The plural society and its enemies: Race and religion in South-East Asia, p. 29.

Tinker, H. (1974). *A new system of slavery: The export of Indian labour overseas, 1830–1920*. London: Oxford University Press.

Tomlins, C. (2001). The legal cartography of colonialization: English intrusions on the American mainland in the seventeenth century. *Law and Social Inquiry*, *26*, 315–372.

U.S. Census Bureau. (1860). Recapitulation: Population of the states and territories by color and condition, with the rate of increase and representation in Congress. Retrieved from www.census.gov/library/publications/1864/dec/1860a.html

Williams, E. (1942). *History of the people of Trinidad and Tobago*. Brooklyn, NY: A and B Publishing Group.

Case Cited

United States v. Rogers, 45 U.S. 4 How. 567 (United States Supreme Court, 1846).

3 The Rule of Law and Its Significance

Rule of Law and Rule by Law in British Colonies

The difference between law that seeks to hold even the powerful accountable and law as an instrument of authoritarian rule is what this book distinguishes as the difference between the rule of law and rule by law. British colonies contained a fundamental contradiction in their governance. On the one hand, Britain governed itself through the rule of law. Aspects of the rule of law also filtered through to colonies, and especially colonies with a large proportion of white settlers among their populations. On the other hand, Britain also imposed a heavy hand when governing its colonies so that colonial rule often took the form of rule by law rather than rule of law. In the 13 American colonies, a similar contradiction arose between the rule of law that white settlers expected for themselves as compared to the rule by law that they applied to imported slaves.

The contradiction between rule of law and rule by law applied across the British Empire even after the American Revolution. In her insightful book *India in the Shadows of Empire: A Legal and Political History 1774–1950*, Mithi Mukherjee (2010b) points to the contradiction in how the British ruled India. The departure point for Professor Mukherjee's analysis is the 1788 impeachment trial of Warren Hastings, the Governor General of the East India Company, on charges of "corruption, use of political power for extorting bribes from native rulers of India, abuse of judicial authority, despotism, and arbitrary rule" (Mukherjee, 2010b, p. 6). She points out that, even as the English East India Company conquered and dominated India, and applied law as an instrument of authoritarian rule over the indigenous peoples, it was being held accountable to Parliament through the rule of law for exceeding the bounds of its legal authority.

British colonial rule was striking in its use of law as an instrument of control (for a range of examples, see, e.g., Leong, 1990; Comaroff, 2001; Hussain, 1999; and Mukherjee, 2010b). Law was especially important for economic reasons. British colonial law in the 13 American colonies and elsewhere in the empire included legal rules to ensure collection of revenues for the Crown. British rule also meant adopting laws and court systems that defined the rules underpinning commercial practices; trade and exploitation of natural resources of a colony required contract law, land titles, mortgages, and other British legal importations rather than the indigenous legal system. As Sven Beckert observes in his magisterial work *The Empire of Cotton*, "The 'law' became particularly important when it came to the actual transformation of the global countryside into a supplier of industrial raw materials and a market for manufactured goods" (Beckert, 2015, p. 236). Law helped to define commercial rights and responsibilities and patterns of doing business, thereby increasing the ability of producers, merchants, manufacturers, and shippers to rely on one another and reduce the costs of doing business across the empire.

Colonial rule systematically increased divisions among racial and ethnic groups. One major difficulty was the way that law could harden divisions in a society by defining them with legal principles, having a disparate impact on each social group. In particular, and important from the perspective of the present book, law formalized and set the terms of white supremacy. While prejudice against black people existed from the time they were brought to American shores, the law ensured and defined the conditions of their inferior status (Degler, 1959). Particular legal restrictions varied by colony and the purpose for which employment of non-whites was encouraged, but the assertion of white superiority and dominance was similar across the British Empire (e.g., Shamir & Hacker, 2001; Stockwell, 1982). Race-based laws included:

> legislation that withheld education from nonwhites, submitted them to special forms of taxation, and denied them the use of liquor, employment on public works, access to goldfields, and even the right to run a business. In South Africa, Indians were required to carry passes, forbidden to use the sidewalks, and relegated to special locations. Everywhere non-whites were deprived of equal

> treatment before the law, were harried and exposed to every manner of indignity.
>
> (Huttenback, 1976, p. 323, footnote omitted)

The racist pattern of British law in the colonial setting can be generalized across British colonies (e.g., Kolsky, 2005; Muendo, 2017; Brückenhaus, 2016). Law Professor Peter-Wesley Smith has written about colonial Hong Kong, for instance, that, "There is no doubt that racism has had significant consequences for social life throughout Hong Kong's history," adding that "In legislation regarding law and order appear some of the most notorious specimens of anti-Chinese statutes" (Wesley-Smith, 1994, pp. 91–95, footnotes omitted). These laws included punishments directed specifically to Chinese individuals, compulsory registration of Chinese people, and a series of laws requiring Chinese people to carry passes, issued by the superintendent of police, if they were found outside their own homes at night (e.g., Wesley-Smith, 1994, p. 96). Christopher Munn adds that the imposition of English law and the English language in Hong Kong colonial courts was quite different from the workings of the law in England. For people subject to colonial rule, for instance in colonial Hong Kong (Munn, 2011) or India (Edwardes, 1976, p. 107), imposition of order on local people was paramount, while doing justice was haphazard at best.

British use of law to enforce dominance tended to have effects even after the British withdrew and ended formal colonialism for a country (Halliday, Karpik, & Feeley, 2012). The contradiction between rule of law and rule by law, which permeated American colonial and post-colonial laws that provided legal protections for whites and applied harsh rules to black slaves, also contributed to the tensions leading to the American Revolution. While Parliament was prepared to impose rule by law on the 13 American colonies if necessary,[1] American colonists believed that they were entitled to the rule of law, including the right to participate in legislative decisions, because their identities as white settlers qualified them:

> What was at stake in the measures taken by the metropolitan government during the 1760s was the entitlement of American settlers to the English system of law and liberties and to the English/British identity implicit in that system. By effectively treating them as a category of others – as if they were savages or slaves – the

> British authorities called into question their entitlement to their inherited rights . . . and thus their very identities as English/British peoples.
>
> (Greene, 2002, p. 260)

The settlers were not content to be placed on the lower side of the plural society divide, and their answer was the American Revolution.

The Importance of the Rule of Law

Writing in the nineteenth century, jurist Albert Venn Dicey rejuvenated the term "rule of law." For Dicey, the rule of law included "at least three distinct though kindred conceptions": (1) "[N]o man is punishable . . . except for a distinct breach of law established in the ordinary legal manner before the ordinary Courts of the land"; (2) "no man is above the law, but . . . every man, whatever be his rank or condition, is subject to the ordinary law of the realm and amenable to the jurisdiction of the ordinary tribunals"; and (3) "the general principles of the constitution (as for example the right to personal liberty, or the right of public meeting) are with us [as] the result of judicial decisions determining the rights of private persons in particular cases brought before the Courts" (Dicey, 1915, pp. 110–115). In other words, for Dicey, the rule of law is based on a set of procedural safeguards of the courts that protect freedoms against arbitrary violation.

Thus, one critical attribute of a government with rule of law is that the government has imposed limits on exercise of its own power. Of course, even under such a system, laws will benefit elites more than others; however, to maintain the legitimation of their rule that a rule of law provides, elites need to share at least some of the benefits and can't simply take all of them for themselves (Thompson, 1975).

Professor Tom R. Tyler (1990) helps to show the fundamental differences between the rule of law and rule by law. He presents a typology of the reasons why people obey the law: on the one hand, the costs of not complying may be greater than the benefits. On the other hand, people may obey because they perceive the law, the legal process (what Tyler calls "procedural justice"), and the legal system as being legitimate. Legitimacy means that people have a sense of obligation to obey commands of a legal system, even if they may sometimes disagree with particular laws, so long as the legal authority is acting within appropriate limits.

In the colonial plural society, the class on top was likely to perceive its legal system as the rule of law and legitimate, while the force of law (i.e., rule by law) was the reason why disfavored groups complied with the colonial order. Thus, the legal system of a colonial plural society can be considered to consist of a rule of law that is seen as legitimate by those on top but may be felt as sheer injustice by those at the bottom.

Laws relating to slavery in the British Empire, and in the 13 American colonies in particular, reflect the contradiction between the formality of a rule of law for the dominant whites and the realities of colonial racism and autocratic domination for enslaved blacks. In autocratic hands (compare, Scheppele, 2018; or Rajah, 2012), a nominal rule of law may meet all relevant criteria but be reduced to a set of hollow formalities. Numerous authoritarian governments that govern through rule by law seek to claim legitimacy despite not governing through the rule of law. In the colonial context, at least for the favored white settler population, the law became an instrument to shape a plural society and assert dominance within it.

White settlers in the 13 American colonies benefited from the rule of law: in the American Revolution white colonists sought and obtained more complete rights to help set the terms of laws that governed them. Rule of law gains legitimacy from the perception of those whom the law governs, that they have a stake in the content of the laws and can affect that content. By contrast, rule by law governed African slaves in the colonies; they had essentially no ability to shape the terms of laws that they were required to obey.

A good way to understand the English, and then British, antecedents of the rule of law governing American colonial settlers is to consider British jurist Sir Frederick Pollock and his essay on "The History of English Law as a Branch of Politics" (1961, pp. 185–211). The essay begins with the tension between King John and his barons that led to the Magna Carta and follows with the English Civil War and the long periods of tension between Parliament and the Crown, leading up to the flight of James II and the ascension of William and Mary. The English Bill of Rights that emerged "was an exercise in political power to ensure that the legal securities for freedom and good government should be fully, fairly, and actively maintained in force" (Pollock, 1961, p. 207).

In his brilliant essay on the rule of law, E. P. Thompson (1975, pp. 258–269) built on the idea that law reflects political outcomes. Thompson conceded to his erstwhile Marxist colleagues that the substance of the law reflects the interests of the ruling class. But, Thompson argued, the logic of the law and the manner in which legal reasoning sets forth principles of general application mean that that logic and those principles also defend the interests of the lower classes. Property rights, for instance, may serve the ruling class well but also protect the smallholder. Law legitimates the rule and interests of the ruling class, but, in so doing, also protects lower classes' lesser interests against arbitrary power.

The form of government affects the way that politics plays out in a rule-of-law system. The framers of the U.S. Constitution sought to ensure that politics would affect law over a long time horizon rather than immediately. Thus, the House of Representatives that faces election every two years can represent the politics and passions of the moment. The U.S. Senate, with six-year terms and one-third of the seats up for election every two years, applies a longer time horizon. In between is the United States President, who faces an election every four years. The United States Supreme Court, with its members appointed for life terms, potentially can take a view with the longest time horizon.

One aspect of the way that law is applied derives from whether an independent judge makes the law through a judicial decision and thus contributes to the development of common law principles, or whether a governing body such as the U.S. Congress, the British Parliament, or a state legislature makes law by enacting legislation. Martin Chanock (1989) argues that statutes (i.e., laws enacted by a legislative body) rather than common law principles often prescribe the disparate treatment of the strata of a plural society.[2] This was seen in American statutes, for example, that prescribed conditions of slavery in great detail.

By contrast, when judges in a judicial case apply common law principles, the result sometimes can mitigate the impact of harsh statutory enactments.[3] Depending on the legal context, on occasion there may be a magnificent decision such as *Sommerset v. Stewart* (discussed in Chapter 4) that in 1772 declared that, once on English soil, an escaped slave could not forcibly be returned to his or her American master. Or there may be a legally reasoned but over-reaching case with appalling implications such as *Dred Scott v. Sandford*, in 1857 (also discussed in Chapter 4) that helped to precipitate the crisis of the Union before the Civil War.

Differing Meanings of the Term "Rule of Law"

Over time, the content of the idea of a "rule of law" has become subject to considerable disagreement among theorists and practitioners. Professor Brian Tamanaha argues that "The rule of law, at its core, requires that government officials and citizens be bound by and act consistent with the law" (Tamanaha, 2009, p. 3). As Tamanaha (2009, p. 14) points out, this conception of the rule of law can encompass both democratic and authoritarian legal systems: "The rule of law does not in itself require democracy, respect for human rights, or any particular content in the law."

This is a critical point. Legal theorist Joseph Raz notes that the general idea of rule of law has been invoked by a range of writers who seek to import expansive values into its content:

> If the rule of law is the rule of the good law then to explain its nature is to expound a complete social philosophy. But if so the term lacks any useful function. We have no need to be converted to the rule of law just to discover that to believe in it is to believe that good should triumph. [The rule of law] is not to be confused with democracy, justice, equality (before the law or otherwise), human rights of any kind or respect for persons or the dignity of man.
>
> (Raz, 2009, p. 211)

In the colonial context, politics and political power meant British superiority and British imposition of a governance structure on subject peoples. In the 13 American colonies, full political authority after the American Revolution passed from Britain to the ruling white settlers and not to black slaves.[4] It was among the settlers that American politics shaped American law. For over two centuries, even when formally emancipated after the Civil War, slaves and former slaves lacked political power and the ability to shape that law.

Thus, rule of law, while a useful concept, at least for some societies,[5] does not include many of the attributes of a democratic society. The fundamental wrongs committed under the colonial and post-colonial systems of slavery and servitude do not negate the fact that the Anglo-American tradition of the rule of law had meaning and importance. As this book seeks to show, it was precisely the tradition of the rule of law that enabled the United States to move beyond the injustices of the plural society and slavery in ways that many other colonies and former colonies without a strong rule of law could not achieve.

With the scope of the rule of law in mind, the question returns: how did the British colonial plural society create such fundamentally different legal rules for white settlers and black slaves? Or, how could the majestic language of freedom in the Declaration of Independence and later in the Constitution of the United States exist alongside the conditions of slavery that were built into the American legal system? Two quite different lines of analysis help shed light on these questions. One relates to Germany under National Socialist rule. This is the conception of the dual state and, by extension, a dual legal system. Ernst Fraenkel, who fled National Socialism to come to the United States, wrote a classic analysis, *The Dual State: A Contribution to the Theory of Dictatorship* (1941). Fraenkel sought to understand a contradiction inherent in the totalitarian state. On the one hand, the National Socialist Party (NSDAP) demanded complete power to dominate the society, economy, and legal system and assert and enforce arbitrary rules. On the other hand, society and the economy needed to function according to bureaucratic, judicial, and other rules and policies so that parties, say to a contract, could understand their respective rights and obligations: "One of the basic propositions of Max Weber's works is that a rational legal system is indispensable for the operation of a capitalistic economic order" (Fraenkel, 1941, p. XIV).

The conflict could be resolved, Fraenkel found, if one recognized that there was a dual legal system. The established civil law system operated as before, except that the NSDAP could arbitrarily intervene at will to change the terms of the civil law (such as with the Nuremberg Laws), to dictate the outcome of judicial proceedings, or simply to apply arbitrary force. The relevance of the dual state and dual legal system to British colonialism in America can be seen in Fraenkel's description of how it worked:

> Viewed sociologically, the Dual State is characterized by the fact that the ruling class assents to the absolute integration of state power on the following conditions:
>
> 1. That those actions which are relevant to its economic situation be regulated in accordance with laws which they consider satisfactory,
> 2. That the subordinate classes, after having been deprived of the protection of the law, be economically disarmed.
>
> (1941, p. 154)[6]

Building on Fraenkel's work, political theorist Judith Shklar articulated how the dual state could exclude an entire class of people from the benefits of Dicey's "rule of law":

> [T]he modern "dual state" . . . may have a perfectly fair and principled private law system, and also a harsh, erratic criminal control system, but it is a "dual state" because some of its population is simply declared to be subhuman, and a public danger, and as such excluded from the legal order entirely.
>
> (Shklar, 1987, p. 2)

The rule of law relating to slavery was just as pernicious. Once the legal system posited that slaves were property, statutes of the American colonies specified conditions of slavery in great detail (as will be discussed in Chapter 4).

Another line of political theory also explains how colonial law could display aspects of Dicey's rule of law and also countenance extreme brutality. This is the law relating to a "state of emergency" that the ruling class believes would threaten law and order and the well-being of the state. Nasser Hussain begins his exploration of a "Jurisprudence of Emergency" by trying to understand the Amritsar massacre of 1919 (also known as the Jallianwala Bagh massacre) in Imperial India, when British General R. E. H. Dyer ordered his troops to fire on peaceful demonstrators, killing hundreds and wounding thousands more. The massacre ended only after the troops nearly ran out of ammunition. Hussain seizes on Dyer's justification for the act as being necessary to teach Indian colonial subjects to respect law and order: "I fired and continued to fire until the crowd dispersed, and I consider this the least amount of firing which would produce the necessary moral and widespread effect it was my duty to produce if I was to justify my action" (Hussain, 1999, p. 95).

Hussain concludes:

> Martial law seeks to effect not just the restoration of order but the restoration of the general authority of the state. In doing so, it takes advantage of the absence of normative constraints on power not just to punish more – which it may or may not do – but to punish out of a different logic. . . . [T]he real need for martial law is not merely to put down this or that transgression, but to restore [the general authority of the state].
>
> (1999, pp. 111–112)

The literature on slavery in the American South is replete with mention of whites who sought to dominate a large population of black slaves. There, as at Amritsar later, the jurisprudence of emergency, backed by fear that the legally prescribed order could be lost, led to application of unrestrained force to protect the system imposed by the dominant group.

Another line of inquiry is relevant to the interplay of the rule of law with a divided colonial and post-colonial society. That is the work of Rogers Smith (1997) on the laws of citizenship (i.e., laws that a society applies to determine who will be considered to belong). His major work, *Civic Ideals: Conflicting Visions of Citizenship in U.S. History*, traces the uneven progress of American citizenship laws from colonial times to the present in becoming increasingly inclusive in counting minorities and women as being accepted full-fledged members of the society. It is by considering citizenship laws in the context of the American rule of law that an answer emerges to the question of why the U.S. was more successful than many other former colonies in finally eroding major barriers posed by a plural society. The answer is that the U.S. has had a rule of law that could help to frame and provide a context for the particular citizenship laws that evolved from excluding to including African Americans and finally to providing African Americans more complete privileges and immunities of citizenship.

The American Constitution and the Rule of Law

After independence, the United States adopted a two-step approach to ensuring the rule of law. First, in 1789, the United States adopted a written Constitution containing numerous checks on the federal government, including the creation of three branches of government, separation of powers among the branches, establishment of the Congress as the preeminent branch with detailed powers specified in Article I, distribution of powers between states and the federal government, and specification of the Bill of Rights to further delimit powers of the federal government. As Lawrence Friedman (1973, pp. 102–103) concludes,

> The federal Constitution was marvelously supple, put together with great political skill. The stability of the country – Civil War crisis aside – has been the main source of its amazing survival. But the Constitution itself deserves a share of the credit. It turned out to be neither too tight nor too loose. It was in essence a frame, a

> skeleton, an outline of the form of government; it mostly held its tongue on specifics.

The second step also was important. To help ensure that the Constitution would be an effective document rather than merely a set of lofty aspirations, the founding generation established a process of judicial review. That meant that courts, and ultimately the Supreme Court, could hear cases that would test laws and executive branch actions against the limitations that the Constitution sets forth, and determine their validity. If the court found that a law or executive branch action violated the Constitution, then the court either could apply a remedy to shape the law or action to be consistent with the Constitution, or, if that were not possible, it could invalidate the law or action entirely.

In his survey of the political history of the Supreme Court's application of judicial review, Professor Barry Friedman (2009) identifies an important pattern: in the years since the Supreme Court decision in *Marbury v. Madison* (1803) that first held a congressional statute unconstitutional, the Supreme Court has had to wield its authority with a careful eye on popular opinion. In cases where the court has failed, such as in decisions in the 1930s striking down New Deal legislation, the court has faced such threatening political backlash that it has had to back down completely. Yet, even in such cases, Professor Friedman finds that the public supported the process of judicial review even while objecting to particular decisions. Popular disapproval thus ended President Franklin Roosevelt's "court packing" plan – seen as an executive over-reaction – while the court responded by becoming more accommodating to New Deal legislation.

Professor Friedman considers the court's application of judicial review to be a fundamental part of the political process that helps to work out the basic tension between a democratic government and a Constitution that limits what popular majorities and their representatives may do:

> [Judicial review] serves as a catalyst for the American people to debate as a polity some of the most difficult and fundamental issues that confront them. It forces the American people to work to reach answers to these questions, to find solutions – often compromises – that obtain broad and lasting support. And it is only when the people have done so that the Court tends to come into

> line with public opinion. . . . This then is the function of judicial review: to serve as a catalyst, to force public debate, and ultimately to ratify the American people's considered views about the meaning of their Constitution.
>
> (B. Friedman, p. 16)

Two lessons emerge from this analysis of judicial review. First, Professor Friedman helps to show the practical significance of legitimacy in validating popular acceptance of laws and executive actions. Legitimacy comes easier in a society governed by rule of law than in a society subject to rule by law. Second, under the Constitution, rule of law remains a stable fixture of American governance. This occurs despite sometimes dramatic variations in the particulars of the law from time to time. As part of the robust political process, both the substance of particular laws and popular perceptions of the legitimacy of those laws may vary considerably over time. In terms of this book, particular laws may change according to the vagaries of the political process, but the rule of law continues to provide the stability that the U.S. has needed both to try to remove the legal barriers of the plural society and also to build new norms of democratic inclusion into the American culture.

Legal scholar Alexander Bickel (1955) addressed the issue of constitutional stability in a brilliant analysis of the 1954 U.S. Supreme Court decision in *Brown v. Board of Education*, a case that added an unprecedented dimension to the Fourteenth Amendment. Bickel saw that the Constitution was designed so that the important question of the legality of racial segregation under the Fourteenth Amendment to the Constitution, which Congress enacted in 1866 and that was ratified in 1868, was

> deferred, left open, to be decided another day. . . . Some no doubt felt more certain than others that the new amendment would make possible further strides toward the ideal of equality. That remained to be decided, and there is no indication of the way in which anyone thought the decision would go on any given specific issue. It depended a good deal on the trend in public opinion.
>
> (Bickel, 1955, pp. 63–64, footnotes omitted)

In this, Bickel says, the Congress of the day may have "emulated the technique of the original framers, who were also responsible to an electorate only partly receptive to the fullness of their principles, and who similarly avoided the explicit grant of some powers without foreclosing their future assumption" (p. 65). Bickel shows how the American constitutional system gives the society room to grow: *Brown v. Board of Education* was properly decided, he says, "because the record of history, properly understood, left the way open to, in fact invited, a decision based on the moral and material state of the nation in 1954, not 1866."[7]

Law professor Stephen Holmes makes a similar point about the way that framers of the Constitution helped to structure and channel decision-making while allowing future generations the discretion to meet unforeseen conditions:

> To satisfy rival interests and muster majority support, participants at the Federal Convention incorporated conflicting and ambiguous provisions into the Constitution, thus delegating essential discretionary powers to their descendants. They deliberately strove to avoid sacrificing posterity to their own limited foresight.
>
> (Holmes, 1995, p. 161, footnote omitted)

The rule of law and American legal institutions thus have provided a framework to allow the evolution of rules of citizenship in the U.S. By contrast, many other former colonies around the world have had a twofold task in trying to overcome their plural societies: they first must build a rule-of-law structure strong enough to deal with the potentially disruptive issue of defining citizenship to include previously excluded groups, and only then can they enact more inclusive citizenship laws that people would be expected to respect.

Few states possess the power needed to force people to dismantle the barriers of a plural society, and the record of post-Civil War Reconstruction in the defeated American South, when the North kept troops on the ground, provides a clear example of the limitations of raw force. What the rule of law adds is the possibility that successful appeals to legitimacy can be codified in ways that allow greater inclusiveness and progressive dismantling of barriers of a plural society. It is important to distinguish the content of particular laws from the rule of law itself. The haphazard progress of American civil rights reflects laws and court decisions that have emerged from the vagaries of the political process. Following Professor Friedman's logic, this very lack of consistency can be seen as a sign of flexibility and strength rather than a weakness of the American rule of law.

As did Furnivall, Matthew Holden looks at the plural society in America from a public administration point of view (Holden, 1996). In the long struggle to overcome restrictions of the plural society, administrative capacity played a key role. During much of the post-Civil War effort to improve conditions of African Americans in the southern states, the North, even when favorably inclined, generally lacked the administrative capacity to enforce requirements to disestablish well-defended elements of the plural society in the South.

A public administration perspective becomes important when one considers the importance of closing the gap between the letter of the law and how the law operates in practice. The rule of law can become meaningful only when it is reflected in the culture and actions of those to whom the law applies. Lacking effective implementation of the rule of law, some societies may move to application of rule by law or to outright lawless violence.

This pattern was especially pronounced after the end of Reconstruction in the American South. As C. Vann Woodward (1966, pp. 86–89) documents, southern elites encouraged lynchings and other cruel violence against black people whom Reconstruction had enfranchised for the first time. Southern elites also moved to restore the system of rule by law over black Americans that Reconstruction had disrupted (Foner, 1988, p. 588). Over time, a significant development occurred: as post-Reconstruction white rule by law over blacks gained strength and became widely implemented in the South, the incidence of lynchings and other violence against black people diminished (Clarke, 1998, p. 283). The incidence of racial violence in the South diminished yet further as the rule of law finally began to take greater hold in the latter half of the twentieth century (Clarke, 1998, p. 289).

The importance of meaningful implementation of the rule of law becomes clear in reviewing antidiscrimination laws in former Portuguese and Spanish colonies in Latin America. Spanish and Portuguese colonies in Latin America never formed rigidly divided societies such as the United States endured. Historian Carl Degler points out how the small number of Portuguese ruling over a much larger population of African slaves in colonial Brazil led to the creation of a large mulatto stratum in the society. What Degler calls a "Mulatto escape hatch" meant that Brazil never formed the type of strictly stratified plural society found in the United States. In other words, importation of African laborers did not create a plural society in Brazil or in Spanish colonies and the successor countries. As Degler writes (p. 5), "Brazilian colonial laws often discriminated against blacks, too, but the systematic separation of the races, whether legally or customarily, is a North American phenomenon."

In Brazil, discrimination bases itself on a combination of color and class. While mulattos have risen in Brazilian society to an extent unfamiliar in the United States before the Civil Rights Movement (Degler, 1971, pp. 104–107, 219, 226–232), race-based discrimination continues. Professor Robert Cottrol finds the same racial pattern also in former Spanish Latin American colonies:

> Let's be clear, racism and racial exclusion are very much a part of the culture in Latin America. . . . But there are important differences as well. Perhaps the most important of these is that race is seen not as a binary divide but as a continuum.
>
> (Cottrol, 2013, p. 11)

It should have been easier in Latin America to end racial discrimination and exclusion than what happened in the United States, which had to deal with overcoming an actual Furnivall-type plural society. Yet, the inability of post-colonial Latin American countries to implement laws about racial discrimination means that they continue to manifest actual racial discrimination to a greater extent than does the United States today. In the United States there has been "a more thoroughgoing civil rights revolution than has occurred to date in Latin America. This revolution has included the development of a more effective body of antidiscrimination law and remedial policies, including often highly contested affirmative action measures" (Cottrol, 2013, pp. 13–14).

Even though their colonial history had not led to such a rigid division of the races as had occurred in the United States, weak legal traditions have made it hard after their independence for Latin American countries to overcome racial barriers. Again, Professor Cottrol says:

> [In Latin America] the quest for a legal regime capable of providing sustained and continuous pressure likely to root out centuries-old patterns of racial exclusion is likely to be elusive. . . . The law is placed on the books but it frequently becomes effectively meaningless. It is part of a broader issue of the problematic nature of the rule of law in the region, a rule or unrule of law that can leave

> significant and at times even expected gaps between the law as it is stated and as it is actually applied.
>
> (Cottrol, 2013, p. 290; see also O'Donnell, 1999)

The importance of implementation also continues to be a recurring issue in the application of the rule of law to help disestablish the plural society in the United States. To be successful, the rule of law needs to facilitate acceptance of the legal system as legitimate so that laws have more of a chance actually to affect the behavior of the people who are supposed to obey them. With the importance of the rule of law in mind, it is appropriate to examine the role of law in defining American society from colonial times to the present and to explore how the rule of law has helped American society to come to where it is today.

Notes

1. For the perspective of the British government, see, e.g., Conway (1998, pp. 325–346).
2. This occurred, for example, in colonial South Africa in the period 1902–1929:

   The South African state was characterised from its beginnings by its immensely detailed statutes, and the huge range of discretionary powers they gave. These were the instruments with which the white elites set about the determined intervention in, re-structuring and domination of, the economy and society. It is the "rule of law" created by the statutory regime, supported by the semi-military police force and the huge network of courts and tribunals, that needs to be analysed without being portrayed as imperfectly legal, or as pretence, or as legitimating.(Chanock, 1989, pp. 268–269)
3. This occurred during the early application of the Black Codes in the American South after the Civil War:

   Once in the hands of local legal professionals, even highly discriminatory legislative enactments became subject to the logic of local legal culture. (Waldrep, 1996, p. 1427)
4. One indicator: The Naturalization Act of 1790, 1 stat. 103, allowed only "any alien, being a free white person," to apply for naturalization to become a U.S. citizen.
5. See, e.g., Tamanaha (2011, p. 245) concerning efforts to establish rule of law in countries where it has not evolved indigenously. ("There is general agreement . . . that establishing the rule of law is a long-term project which no one knows how to accomplish.")
6. Fraenkel wrote his book at the end of the 1930s (i.e., before full dimensions of the Holocaust were apparent).
7. By the end of the Warren Court, Professor Bickel had lost his optimism about the ability of the Supreme Court to effect change. For a good synopsis and response, see Lewis (1969).

Sources Cited

Beckert, S. (2015). *Empire of cotton: A global history*. New York, NY: Alfred A. Knopf.

Bickel, A. M. (1955). The original understanding and the segregation decision. *Harvard Law Review*, *69*(1), 1–65.

Brückenhaus, D. (2016). Identifying colonial subjects: Fingerprinting in British Kenya, 1900–1960. *Geschichte und Gesellschaft*, *42*(1), 60–85. doi:10.13109/gege.2016.42.1.60

Chanock, M. (1989). Writing South African legal history: A prospectus. *Journal of African History*, *30*(2), 265–288.

Clarke, J. W. (1998). Without fear or shame: Lynching, capital punishment and the subculture of violence in the American South. *British Journal of Political Science*, *28*(2), 269–289.

Comaroff, J. L. (2001). Symposium introduction: Colonialism, culture, and the law: A forward. *Law and Social Inquiry*, *26*(2), 305–314.

Conway, S. (1998). Britain and the revolutionary crisis, 1763–1791. In *The Oxford history of the British empire: Vol. II: The eighteenth century* (pp. 325–346). Oxford: Oxford University Press.

Cottrol, R. J. (2013). *The long lingering shadow: Slavery, race, and law in the American hemisphere*. Athens, GA: University of Georgia Press.

Degler, C. N. (1959). Slavery and the genesis of American race prejudice. *Comparative Studies in Society and History*, *2*(1), 49–66.

Degler, C. N. (1971). *Neither black nor white: Slavery and race relations in Brazil and the United States*. Madison, WI: University of Wisconsin Press.

Dicey, A. V. (1915). *Introduction to the study of the law of the constitution* (8th ed.). London: Macmillan; reprinted Indianapolis, IN: Liberty Classics, 1982.

Edwardes, M. (1976). *British India, 1772–1947: A survey of the nature and effects of alien rule*. Calcutta: Rupa and Company.

Foner, E. (1988). *Reconstruction: America's unfinished revolution, 1863–1877*. New York, NY: Harper and Row.

Fraenkel, E. (1941). *The dual state: A contribution to the theory of dictatorship* (E. A. Shils, E. Lowenstein, & K. Knorr, Trans.). New York, NY: Oxford University Press.

Friedman, B. (2009). *The will of the people: How public opinion has influenced the Supreme Court and shaped the meaning of the constitution*. New York, NY: Farrar, Straus and Giroux.

Friedman, L. M. (1973). *A history of American law*. New York, NY: Simon and Shuster.

Greene, J. P. (2002). By their laws shall ye know them: Law and identity in colonial British America. *The Journal of Interdisciplinary History*, *33*(2) 247–260.

Halliday, T. C., Karpik, L., & Feeley, M. M. (2012). *Fates of political liberalism in the British post-colony: The politics of the legal complex*. New Delhi: Cambridge University Press.

Holden, M., Jr. (1996). Public administration and the plural society. *Continuity ontinuity and disruption: Essays in public administration*. Pittsburgh, PA: University of Pittsburgh Press.

Holmes, S. (1995). *Passions and constraint: On the theory of liberal democracy*. Chicago, IL: University of Chicago Press.

Hussain, N. (1999). Towards a jurisprudence of emergency: Colonialism and the rule of law. *Law and Critique*, *10*, 93–115.

Huttenback, R. A. (1976). *Racism and empire: White settlers and colored immigrants in the British self-governing colonies, 1830–1910*. Ithaca, NY: Cornell University Press.

Kolsky, E. (2005). Codification and the rule of colonial difference: Criminal procedure in British India. *Law and History Review*, *23*(3), 631–683.

Leong, A. P. B. (1990). *The development of Singapore law: Historical and socio-legal perspectives*. Singapore: Butterworths.

Lewis, A. (1969, October 10). The heavenly city of professor Bickel. *New York Times*, p. 46.

Muendo, M. (2017, March 15). Kenyans are still oppressed by archaic colonial laws. *The Conversation*.

Mukherjee, M. (2010b). *India in the shadows of empire: A legal and political history 1774–1950*. New Delhi: Oxford University Press.

Munn, C. (2011). *Anglo-China: Chinese people and British rule in Hong Kong, 1841–1880*. Hong Kong: Hong Kong University Press.

O'Donnell, G. (1999). Polyarchies and the (un)rule of law in Latin America: A partial conclusion. In J. E. Mendez, G. O'Donnell, & P. S. Pinheiro (Eds.), *The (un)rule of law and the underprivileged in Latin America* (pp. 303–337). Notre Dame, IN: University of Notre Dame Press.

Pollock, S. F. (1961). *Jurisprudence and legal essays by Sir Frederick Pollock*. New York, NY: St. Martin's Press.

Rajah, J. (2012). *Authoritarian rule of law: Legislation, discourse, and legitimacy in Singapore*. Cambridge: Cambridge University Press.

Raz, J. (2009). *The authority of law: Essays on law and morality* (2nd ed.). New York, NY: Oxford University Press.

Scheppele, K. L. (2018). Autocratic legalism. *University of Chicago Law Review*, *85*(2), pp. 545–583.

Shamir, R., & Hacker, D. (2001). Colonialism's civilizing mission: The case of the Indian hemp drug commission. *Law and Social Inquiry*, *26*(2), 435–461.

Shklar, J. N. (1987). Political theory and the rule of law. In A. Hutchinson & P. Monahan (Eds.), *The rule of law or ideology*. Toronto: Carswell.

Smith, R. M. (1997). *Civic ideals: Conflicting visions of citizenship in U.S. history*. New Haven, CT: Yale University Press.

Stockwell, A. J. (1982). The white man's burden and brown humanity: Colonialism and ethnicity in British Malaya. *Southeast Asian Journal of Social Science*, *10*(1), 44–68.

Tamanaha, B. Z. (2009). A concise guide to the rule of law. In G. Palombella & N. Walker (Eds.), *Relocating the rule of law* (pp. 3–15). Portland, OR: Hart Publishing.

Tamanaha, B. Z. (2011). The primacy of society and the failures of law and development. *Cornell International Law Journal*, *44*(2), 216–247.

Thompson, E. P. (1975). *Whigs and hunters: The origin of the Black Act*. New York, NY: Pantheon Books.

Tyler, T. R. (1990). *Why people obey the law*. New Haven, CT: Yale University Press.

Waldrep, C. (1996). Substituting law for the lash: Emancipation and legal formalism in a Mississippi county court. *The Journal of American History*, *82*(4), 1425–1451.

Wesley-Smith, P. (1994). Anti-Chinese legislation in Hong Kong. In M. K. Chan (Ed.), *Precarious balance: Hong Kong between China and Britain 1842–1992* (pp. 91–105). Armonk, NY: Sharpe.

Woodward, C. V. (1966). *The strange career of Jim Crow* (2nd ed.). New York, NY: Oxford University Press.

Law and Cases Cited

Naturalization Act of 1790, 1 stat. 103 Stat. (1790).

Brown v. Board of Education of Topeka Kansas, 347 U.S. 483, 74 S. Ct. 686, 98 L. Ed. 873 (1954).

Dred Scott v. Sandford, 60 U.S. 393 (1857).

Marbury v. Madison, 5 U.S. 137 (1803).

Sommerset v. Stewart, 98 ER 499 (1772).

4 Law and America's Divided Society

Law, Slavery, and America's Divided Society

As British colonial rule funneled both white settlers and black slaves into different strata of the emerging American divided society, laws developed to distinguish the roles of slaves and their masters (Degler, 1959). Historian Kenneth Morgan concludes:

> A statutory law of race and slavery existed in all thirteen British North American colonies by the middle of the eighteenth century. They gave owners virtually complete control over the movements, fraternization, and behavior of their slave charges. The laws were draconian, allowing for a wide range of physical punishments including . . . the death penalty. . . . Under these laws, slaves lacked various rights – the right to marry, the right to testify in court, the right to challenge the hereditary nature of slavery. Enslaved Africans effectively had no redress against maltreatment by whites.
>
> (Morgan, 2007, p. 113; see also Wiecek, 1977a, p. 259)

South Carolina was an early colony that spelled out terms of the slave-owner relationship in law. The *Fundamental Constitutions of Carolina*, March 1, 1669, drafted at least in part by John Locke,[1] stated that, "Every freeman of Carolina shall have absolute power and authority over his negro slaves, of what opinion or religion soever" (Lillian Goldman Law Library, The Avalon Project, and Yale University Law School, 1669, March 1). The colony also enacted extensive legislation prescribing the terms of slavery and the rules and requirements for slaves (e.g., McCord, 1840).

Judge Leon Higginbotham, Jr. surveyed the law of slavery in England and in six American colonies: Virginia, Massachusetts, New York, South Carolina, Georgia, and Pennsylvania. He saw Virginia as another early colony to spell out the conditions of slavery in law:

> Though by 1700 the Virginia legal system – court and legislature alike – had boxed in the colony's black population, it was not until 1705 that the Virginia legislature passed a comprehensive statute effectively removing blacks from the family of man and reassigning them to the classification of real property.
>
> (Higginbotham, 1978, p. 50)

The 1705 Virginia law permitted owners to kill their slaves if needed to enforce compliance:

> XXXIV. And if any slave resist his master, or owner, or other person, by his or her order, correcting such slave, and shall happen to be killed in such correction, it shall not be accounted felony; but the master, owner, and every such other person so giving correction, shall be free and acquit of all punishment and accusation for the same, as if such incident had never happened: And also, if any negro, mulatto, or Indian, bond or free, shall at any time, lift his or her hand, in opposition against any christian, not being negro, mulatto, or Indian, he or she so offending shall, for every such offence, proved by the oath of the party, receive on his or her bare back, thirty lashes, well laid on; cognizable by a justice of the peace for that county wherein such offence shall be committed.
>
> (Laws of Virginia, 1705, October, p. 459)

The 1705 law also made clear that loss of a slave meant a loss of property to the owner:

> XXXVIII. Provided always, and it is further enacted, That for every slave killed, in pursuance of this act, or put to death by law, the master or owner of such slave shall be paid by the public:
>
> XXXIX. And to the end, the true value of every slave killed, or put to death, as aforesaid, may be the better known; and by that means, the assembly the better enabled to make a suitable allowance thereupon, Be it enacted, That upon application of the master

> or owner of any such slave, to the court appointed for proof of public claims, the said court shall value the slave in money, and the clerk of the court shall return a certificate thereof to the assembly, with the rest of the public claims.

The law was amended in 1727 to specify that slaves would be conveyed as chattels "by will, by deed of gift or of sale" (Hurd, 1858, p. 242).

Judicial redress for slaves was largely unobtainable. In South Carolina, for example, black people were subject to a 1740 law, "for the better ordering and governing of Negroes and other Slaves in this Province." On the one hand, the law subjected slaves to harsh criminal rules and penalties; on the other, slaves lacked individual protections of the common law: "to a large degree, [the law] defined slavery as an absence of rights and slaves as legal non-persons." Thus, slaves could not testify under oath. "This bar rendered slave testimony inadmissible in the General Court where whites were prosecuted, and meant that whites' sworn testimony would be given preference to slaves' unsworn testimony in the magistrates' courts where slaves were tried" (Olwell, 1998, p. 62).

A North Carolina Supreme Court case, *The State v. John Mann*, 13 N.C. 263 (1829), shows the absolute dominance a master could exercise under the law:

> The end [of slavery] is the profit of the master, his security and the public safety; the subject, one doomed in his own person, and his posterity, to live without knowledge, and without the capacity to make any thing his own, and to toil that another may reap the fruits . . . such services can only be expected from one who has no will of his own; who surrenders his will in implicit obedience to that of another. Such obedience is the consequence only of uncontrolled authority over the body. There is nothing else which can operate to produce the effect. The power of the master must be absolute, to render the submission of the slave perfect.

The law continued to expand with continuing growth of the populations of both white settlers and African slaves. An 1837 Pennsylvania case makes clear the strict racial boundaries that formed the American plural society:

> no colored race was party to our social compact . . . our ancestors settled the province as a community of white men, and the blacks

> were introduced into it as a race of slaves; whence an unconquerable prejudice of caste . . . has come down to our day.
>
> (*Hobbs v. Fogg*, 1837)

After the Revolutionary War and experimentation with government under the Articles of Confederation, American delegates met in a Constitutional Convention to deliberate on whether a stronger union might be crafted (e.g., Lacroix, 2010). In the course of deliberations, it became clear that non-slave states would need to make extensive concessions if southern states were to become part of the new union (e.g., Scott, 1893, pp. 582–583).[2] Those concessions helped to enshrine a black-white plural society in America that continued long after Britain itself abolished slavery.

While the Constitution carefully avoided using the word "slavery," historians point to at least eight constitutional provisions that accommodated the interests of slave states:

1. Article I, section 2, provided for apportionment of representatives in the House based on population, including all free persons and three-fifths of the slaves (the "three-fifths" clause); this provided whites in southern slave states additional representation, even though slaves themselves could not vote;
2. Article I, section 2 and Article I, section 9 each required that direct taxes (including capitation taxes) be apportioned among the states, again on the basis of the three-fifths compromise, "the purpose being to prevent Congress from laying a head tax on slaves to encourage their emancipation" (Wiecek, 1977b, p. 62; Finkelman, 1987);
3. Article I, section 9, prohibited the Congress from abolishing the international trade in slaves or the importation of slaves to the United States before 1808;
4. Article IV, section 2, prohibited a state from enacting laws to emancipate fugitive slaves and required that fugitives be returned on demand of the master;
5. Article I, section 8, empowered the Congress to call up state militias to suppress insurrections, including slave uprisings;
6. Article IV, section 4, required the federal government to protect the states against domestic violence, again including slave insurrections;

7. Article V prescribed for the amendment of the Constitution and specified that the provisions of Article I, section 9, clauses 1 and 4 (pertaining to the slave trade and direct taxes) could not be amended before 1808;
8. Article I, section 9 and Article I, section 10 prohibited the federal government and states from taxing exports, "one purpose being to prevent them from taxing slavery indirectly by taxing the exported products of slave labor" (Wiecek, 1977b).

The Constitutional Convention also decided, in Article II, Section 1, that voting in the electoral college "be equal to the whole number of Senators and Representatives to which the State may be entitled in the Congress." Thus, the three-fifths compromise expanded the influence of slave-holding states in selecting the President, at least until the Fourteenth Amendment, passed by Congress in 1866 and ratified in 1868, repealed the three-fifths provision. Reviewing the convention debates, legal historian Paul Finkelman contends that today's electoral college came about as a result of the Founders choosing a method of election that was "weighted in favor of slavery" (Finkelman, 2002, p. 1156). Disproportionate southern political influence before the Civil War extended to much of Congress, many justices of the U.S. Supreme Court, and many U.S. Presidents.

In Britain, the campaign to abolish slavery in the British Empire began in the late eighteenth century, well before the American Civil War. It took time for British opinion to build that the conventional wisdom was wrong and that slavery was an evil that needed to be abolished. The landmark 1772 legal decision *Sommerset v. Stewart*, written by Lord Mansfield of the King's Bench, greatly influenced opinion. Sommerset, an African slave, arrived in England, escaped his American master, and was recaptured. Lord Mansfield ruled that English law did not support the keeping of a slave on English soil and that Sommerset must be freed. Judge Leon Higginbotham explains that *Sommerset* "profoundly influenced American and English legal opinions for decades. Lord Mansfield proclaimed that neither moral nor political grounds existed to support slavery: the institution could be justified only by positive law" (Higginbotham, 1978, p. 313). In other words, slavery was not a natural state of affairs; rather a legislature that enacted laws creating the condition of slavery also could repeal those laws and abolish slavery. While slaves were subject to rule by law, the door could be opened to apply the rule of law and free them. Great Britain bestowed on the American colonies both the evil of slavery and the role model of how to apply the rule of law, once the Civil War had freed the slaves, to include black people as American citizens under the law.

Kenneth Morgan identifies the year 1787 when the change in public opinion had built to the point that organized opposition to slavery began in Britain. That year a predominantly Quaker organization formed, the Society for Effecting the Abolition of the Slave Trade. The society began peppering Parliament and public opinion with information about conditions in the slave trade and proposals for abolition (Morgan, 2007; Drescher, 1994).

Antislavery forces built strength in Parliament but ran into strong opposition from economic interests, including those who argued that without slave labor West Indian sugar would no longer be economic, and the sugar trade would fall into the hands of rival powers. Liverpool and other cities depended on the slave trade economically. Indeed, many slave traders were members of Parliament. Opposition to abolition and emancipation was fierce because of the economic value of slavery to the British Empire:

> Slavery stood at the center of the most dynamic and far-reaching production complex in human history. Herman Merivale, British colonial bureaucrat, noted that Manchester's and Liverpool's "opulence is as really owing to the toil and suffering of the negro, as if his hands had excavated their docks and fabricated their steam engines." Capital accumulation in peripheral commodity production, according to Merivale, was necessary for metropolitan economic expansion, and access to labor, if necessary by coercion, was a precondition for turning abundant lands into productive suppliers of raw materials.
>
> (Beckert, 2015, p. 244)

British legislation to abolish slavery proceeded in stages. The first legislative victory came during the Napoleonic wars with passage of a law to cut off slave traffic to French colonies and other foreign powers. This eliminated about a third of the British slave trade and cleared the way for enactment of legislation in 1807 to end the slave trade entirely.

Ending the slave trade merely ended the transportation of slaves from Africa but did not end the institution of slavery itself. The final emancipation law passed Parliament on July 31, 1833, and became effective one year later. The law included payment of £20 million to planters as compensation for loss of their slaves' labor, and a system of largely unpaid "apprenticeships" for freed slaves that came to an end prematurely in 1838.[3]

The abolition of slavery came to the British Caribbean colonies at a time when increased worldwide competition had diminished demand and seriously reduced prices that British sugar planters could command. To obtain the needed cheap labor, planters imported indentured servants, mostly from India, to work in the sugar cane fields. Nearly 250,000 Indians came to Trinidad, 15,000 to British Guiana, and over 36,000 to Jamaica. The Indian indenture system ended only in 1917, by which time multi-racial divided societies, including whites, people of Asian descent, and people of African descent, were well established in many Caribbean colonies.[4]

From the perspective of the cotton industry, Parliament's abolition of slavery in the empire had little effect. Because the United States were no longer colonies, the southern states, where the large majority of slaves produced cotton for the British textile industry, were not governed by the emancipation of slaves in the British Empire. Southern states became evermore tightly integrated into the British-dominated network of cotton production, textile manufacturing, and sales (Beckert, 2015, p. 204).

In the United States it took a Civil War to end slavery. The two critical issues that the Constitution had failed to resolve, slavery and states' rights, drove a wedge between southern states and the rest of the country until the gap became impossible to bridge. Economic changes lessened the interest of northern manufacturers in preserving slavery, while growing use of wage labor in northern factories showed that slavery was an unnecessary part of the cotton trade. Again, Professor Beckert says:

> American slavery had begun to threaten the very prosperity it produced, as the distinctive political economy of the cotton South collided with the incipient political economy of free labor and domestic industrialization of the North. . . . Ample supplies of fertile land and bonded labor had made the South into [a British] plantation, but by 1860 large numbers of Americans, especially in the northern states, protested such semicolonial dependence.
>
> (2015, p. 245)

The legal basis of slavery became increasingly frustrating to northerners and the growing U.S. abolitionist movement. This reflects the struggle over laws that, from the perspective of the present book, show the centrality of law in the effort to address the divided society left over from the U.S. experience as a British colony. The 1850 Fugitive Slave Act made harboring or concealing a runaway slave a crime, made it a crime for marshals or deputy marshals to refuse to accept and enforce a warrant for the return of a slave, and prohibited the negro from testifying or calling witnesses on his or her behalf. The statute also called for the creation of a system of commissioners to adjudicate claims by slave owners and provided that a commissioner would be compensated $10 if the person were adjudged a runaway slave and turned over to the owner, but only $5 if the petition were adjudged to be false.

Dred Scott v. Sandford (1857) was a decision of the Supreme Court ruling that a slave who was taken by his master to Illinois, a free state, and then to Missouri, a slave state, was not a free person because (1) negroes were not "citizens" within the meaning of the Constitution, (2) therefore lacked the right to bring a lawsuit in federal court, and (3) federal courts thus had no jurisdiction over the case. Moreover, (4) Congress had no power to regulate slavery in territories acquired since the establishment of the United States. Scott then was left subject to a Missouri Supreme Court case that ruled, under Missouri law, Scott had not become free because of the time he had been held in Illinois (Vishneski, 1988).

Together, the 1850 law and *Dred Scott* said explicitly that under the Constitution, while Congress had power to force the return of slaves to their owners, Congress lacked power to end slavery and its cruelties. For many northerners that position was untenable. The election of Abraham Lincoln, a vocal opponent of slavery, and the consequent secession of the southern states precipitated the Civil War, which lasted four years and cost hundreds of thousands of lives.

At the close of the Civil War, and after the untimely death of President Lincoln, the Congress enacted legislation for three Civil Rights amendments to the Constitution. The Thirteenth Amendment, ratified in 1865, abolished slavery and involuntary servitude, except as punishment for a crime; the Fourteenth Amendment, ratified in 1868, contained three important provisions: the Citizenship Clause, which overturned *Dred Scott* and conferred citizenship on "all persons born or naturalized in the United States"; the Due Process Clause, applying due process requirements to state governments; and the Equal Protection Clause, which became especially important a century later to help ensure to all citizens the equal protection of state laws. The Fifteenth Amendment, ratified in 1870, prohibited the federal government and state governments from denying a citizen the right to vote based on that citizen's "race, color, or previous condition of servitude."

Despite losses in the Civil War and the majestic language of these Constitutional amendments, America's travails with the divided society, left over from colonial times, did not end. As textile manufacturing technologies improved, demand for cotton increased as never before. That led the southern elite to find a way to obtain labor of freed slaves on the least costly basis possible.[5] Although slavery was abolished, the law again became an instrument of coercion to ensure that African Americans would produce cotton and would not defect to other livelihoods or other states. The divided society remained intact, at least in the South.

The Divided Society Persists: Post-Civil War Legal Restrictions on Blacks

Many in the South were not yet ready to give up their divided society. The Civil War had caused the loss of one-fifth of the southern adult white male population and massive economic devastation (Foner, 1988, pp. 124–125). Not only was there the imperative to get the economy restarted (Zeichner, 1940), but the freeing of the slaves also led to considerable white resentment, especially among the white planter class (Foner, 1988, pp. 128–136, "Masters without slaves").

As Professor Matthew Holden observes, despite stationing troops in the South after the war, the North lacked the administrative capability to bring the rule of law to emancipated slaves who remained subject to the dominant white population:

> The United States became, after the Civil War, a presumptively free but highly stratified society. The former Confederacy was a territory containing two populations, white and black. The white portion had greater political resources. It also had all the military resources: the police were, after all, the Confederate Army in civilian dress. And the dominant group had no intention of living on terms of formal equality with the other group. If the second

> population, the freed blacks, were to have their condition notably improved, they required an alliance with the federal government. And if those allies were to be effective, they needed an administrative mechanism that they lacked. . . . [After a series of adverse Supreme Court decisions, discussed next] the institutions of force that became pertinent were those of state and local governments in the former Confederacy.
>
> (1996, p. 225, footnote omitted)

To the extent that northern occupation would permit, southern planters sought to bring blacks back to their subordinate social and economic positions. The first phase of restoration was the effort to enact laws, later known as the Black Codes, to force freed slaves back onto plantations to work. On the one hand, the codes allowed blacks to marry, acquire and own property, make contracts, sue and be sued, and testify in cases involving blacks. On the other hand, the codes effectively limited black economic options besides plantation labor by requiring black people to contract for their labor, punishing those who refused to contract, and preventing whites from making competing offers for black labor (Foner, 1988, p. 199).

The nature of the Black Codes can be seen in the Mississippi Vagrant Law:

> All freedmen, free negroes and mulattoes in this State, over the age of eighteen years, found on the second Monday in January, 1866, or thereafter, with no lawful employment or business, or found unlawful assembling themselves together, either in the day or night time, and all white persons assembling themselves with freedmen, free negroes or mulattoes, or usually associating with freedmen, free negroes or mulattoes, on terms of equality, or living in adultery or fornication with a freed woman, freed negro or mulatto, shall be deemed vagrants, and on conviction thereof shall be fined in a sum not exceeding, in the case of a freedman, free negro or mulatto, fifty dollars, and a white man two hundred dollars, and imprisonment at the discretion of the court, the free negro not exceeding ten days, and the white man not exceeding six months. [6]

Of significance here is how, to maintain the structure of a divided society, southern elites needed to apply penalties to restrict whites as well as blacks from crossing the color line. The overt racist intent of the Black Codes offended northern public opinion and officials and forced southern states to change the terms of the laws so that they did not explicitly apply to black people alone (Foner, 1988, p. 209). Although the revised laws no longer mentioned race, they were intended to enforce white control over the labor system and local authorities carried them out with that goal (Cohen, 1976, p. 34).

The new laws created an interlocking set of constraints on black people, including (1) requirements to sign labor contracts or be arrested under vagrancy laws, and (2) if arrested or with unpaid debts, to be indentured to serve as forced labor for private parties who contracted with the locality for convict labor services. Other laws prohibited whites from competing for labor of a black person who was under contract to another white, and severely limited the ability of agents to entice black people to move out of state to seek better working conditions (Cohen, 1976). Extralegal and illegal practices directed at black workers included cruelty that at times was greater than most slaves had been subjected to, especially because, under the new laws, owners no longer had a property interest in conserving the physical strength of the black people working for them (Blackmon, 2009). The result was to require black people in the South to work as sharecroppers, tenants, or contract or convict laborers, under harsh laws and practices that remained in effect until World War II (Cohen, 1976; Russell, 1907, pp. 207–215).

Legal cases in the post-Civil War period eliminated much of the benefit of the Civil Rights amendments and implementing legislation that the Congress had enacted. The Fourteenth Amendment confers citizenship on all persons born or naturalized in the United States and specifies in part that "No state shall make or enforce any law which shall abridge the privileges and immunities of citizens of the United States." In 1873 the U.S. Supreme Court decided the *Slaughterhouse Cases*, a matter that concerned states' rights, but not directly race, discrimination, or white supremacy. The Court's majority adopted such a narrow reading of the scope of the privileges and immunities clause of the Fourteenth Amendment that it precluded federal courts from reviewing the constitutionality of post-Reconstruction efforts by southern states to limit the rights of citizenship of emancipated blacks. In a ringing dissent, Justice Stephen Field argued that U.S. citizenship was a broad concept and that the Fourteenth Amendment should have much broader application: "The privileges and immunities designated are those which of right belong to the citizens of all free governments. Clearly among these must be placed the right to pursue a lawful employment in a lawful manner, without other restraint than such as equally affects all persons."

The subtext of the case was a reluctance to expand jurisdiction of the federal government to subject state laws to constitutional challenge. Had Justice Field been able to carry the majority, it might have been possible to end many southern race laws decades sooner than they ended. From time to time the U.S. Department of Justice did attempt to enforce a federal anti-peonage law against holding a person in involuntary servitude to pay off a debt. While involuntary debt servitude of black people was widespread in the post-Civil War South, the anti-peonage law was difficult to enforce in the context of a southern legal culture that sought ways to avoid its impact, and the effort faded without effect (Blackmon, 2009, chapters VII and VIII; Russell, 1907).

Other U.S. Supreme Court cases constrained application of the civil rights amendments and implementing legislation in a way that, together, allowed southern states to enact evermore sweeping laws to deprive black Americans of voting rights and maintain segregation and the plural society of the South. Major cases included:

- *United States v. Cruikshank* (1876), holding that the Due Process and Equal Protection Clauses of the Fourteenth Amendment applied only to acts of a government or government official, known as "state action," not to acts of individual people;
- *United States v. Reese* (1876), narrowly construing voting rights and enforcement under the Fifteenth Amendment;
- the *Civil Rights Cases* (1883), holding, among other constrictions imposed on the Civil Rights Amendments, that the Civil Rights Act of 1875, banning discrimination in public services, was unconstitutional; and
- *Williams v. Mississippi* (1898), upholding nominally neutral literacy tests and poll taxes as nondiscriminatory.[7]

Then came the Supreme Court decision in *Plessy v. Ferguson* (1896) that permitted outright segregation and established the doctrine of "separate but equal." In that case the court rejected a constitutional challenge to a Louisiana statute that required railway companies to segregate whites and blacks but provide them "equal, but separate" accommodations. Professor Eric Foner notes the consequences:

> The Plessy decision was quickly followed by laws mandating segregation in every aspect of life, from schools to hospitals, waiting rooms to toilets, drinking fountains to cemeteries. In some states, taxi drivers were forbidden by law to carry members of different races at the same time. . . . [S]egregation was part of a complex system of white domination, in which each component – disenfranchisement, unequal economic status, inferior education – reinforced the others.
>
> (Foner, 1999, p. 322)

Even in the early twentieth century, black Americans, although emancipated from slavery, remained subject to rule by law in many places, especially in the South. The United States remained confined by the legal framework of a divided society.

Faced with barriers that southern landowners and their supporters imposed in an effort to maintain as much of the divided society as they could, and the consequent poverty and limited opportunities, American blacks overcame numerous legal and practical obstacles and left the South in droves. Between 1910 and 1940 about 1.5 million black people left for urban centers in the North and West. Between 1940 and 1950 another 1.5 million left. Not only racism drove them out; the tenuous economic position of a sharecropper or tenant farmer, whether white or black, was also a factor (Tolnay & Beck, 1990; Roberts, 2012, pp. 12–38), as were threats of lethal violence and the mediocrity of available public services such as education. Economic factors grew in importance as cotton prices dropped in the Great Depression and the Franklin Roosevelt administration instituted new programs to pay landowners to take agricultural land out of production, thereby reducing demand for agricultural labor.

Unfortunately, escaping the South did not mean immediately escaping discrimination and burdens of the divided society. Indeed, under President Woodrow Wilson, the federal government itself discriminated against hiring black employees (Wolgemuth, 1958; Wolgemuth, 1959). Discrimination came also from fear that incoming blacks would take jobs that whites held (Ash, 1991, p. 58). Major race riots broke out in numerous cities, including East St. Louis, Philadelphia, Chicago,

Baltimore and – especially violently – Tulsa, Oklahoma. "Detroit in June 1943 experienced a race riot that left 34 persons dead and a 'hate strike' of 20,000 auto workers protesting the upgrading of black workers in a plant manufacturing aircraft engines" (Foner, 1999, p. 331). This also was a pattern across British colonies: in many white settler colonies, the arrival of South Asians, Chinese, and other immigrants caused anger and violence when whites feared that their jobs were being displaced (Huttenback, 1973, pp. 75ff.).

In the U.S., laws and government actions created nationwide barriers against living in integrated neighborhoods. The New Deal marked the large-scale entry of the federal government into the housing market. Racial discrimination permeated New Deal programs such as those of the Home Owners Loan Corporation (HOLC) and Federal Housing Administration (FHA) and later the Veterans Administration (VA).

The HOLC was intended to assist homeowners in the Great Depression who faced foreclosure and also to help them reduce the cost of carrying their mortgages. In the two years after its inception in 1933, the HOLC provided over $3 billion to help support over a million mortgages, constituting one-tenth of all U.S. owner-occupied nonfarm residences. However, in providing its support, the HOLC formally discriminated and initiated the practice known as "red lining" (i.e., blocking the flow of funds to minority neighborhoods). HOLC appraisers invariably rated black peoples' neighborhoods in the lowest of four appraisal categories. "The HOLC simply applied [contemporaneous] notions of ethnic and racial worth to real estate appraising on an unprecedented scale. With the assistance of local realtors and banks, it assigned one of its four ratings to every block in every city," and provided its financial support accordingly (Jackson, 1980, pp. 423–424).

From its inception in 1934 to 1972, the FHA provided mortgage insurance to help almost 11 million people to own their homes and provided loan guarantees to help another 22 million people to finance home improvements. The U.S. homeownership rate grew from 44 percent to 63 percent in the same period. Again, however, there was another side to that impressive track record. In its first three decades, only 2 percent of FHA home loans "went to nonwhite applicants" (Krysan & Crowder, 2017, p. 8). As the U.S. National Commission on Urban Problems concluded (1969, p. 101):

> For many years FHA operated with the conventional racial prejudice characteristic of many middle class real estate men. The

> agency's original personnel was primarily recruited from this group in the 1930's. Until 1948, when restrictive covenants or written agreements not to sell to Negroes were declared unconstitutional by the Supreme Court, FHA actually encouraged its borrowers to give such guarantees and was a powerful enforcer of the covenants. The FHA definition of a sound neighborhood was a "homogeneous" one – one that was racially segregated.

One result of these policies, as well as racially motivated local zoning laws and other restrictions, such as legal covenants that prohibited white homeowners from selling their homes to black people, was to divide localities into neighborhoods where white people lived that were separate from neighborhoods where black people lived. The colonial "plural society," as Furnivall labeled it, continued to predominate in the United States.

Other New Deal programs displayed white racial favoritism as well. President Roosevelt, regardless of his personal views, needed to do business with congressional committees dominated by Senators and Representatives from the South. The South had been devastated by the Great Depression and southern leaders supported vast relief programs. But they wanted these programs to be administered by states and localities rather than centrally by the federal government:

> Planters were highly defensive against any direct flow of cash into the system of tenancy that might lessen the dependence of the sharecropper on the landlord. . . . [L]andlords, who were often appointed to administrative positions in local government, manipulated [federal] relief funds in a variety of ways. For example, blacks unilaterally received lower rates of relief than whites in the South, with relief generally kept below the subsistence furnished by the landlord. Not only were rates of relief lower for blacks, but the proportion receiving relief was only half of that for southern whites, even though rates of black poverty were substantially higher. Furthermore, at planters' requests, relief offices in many rural counties were closed during the two months of cotton picking.
>
> (Quagdano, 1988, pp. 242 and 241–242, footnotes omitted)

For the major New Deal program that southern leaders could not prevent from being centralized in the federal government, the Social Security Act of 1935, which created the Social Security program to provide a safety net for the elderly, southern members of Congress were able to exclude agricultural workers, domestic workers, and part-time workers from coverage (Finegold, 1988, pp. 209–210; Quagdano, 1988, p. 238). These were occupations in which black people tended to work, and Old Age Insurance failed to cover a substantial fraction of black people, a problem addressed only in the 1950s and 1960s when regularly employed agricultural and domestic workers were made eligible (Myles, 1988, p. 273).

Assistance programs soon became bifurcated, and the difference became pronounced: "in 1939. . . wives, elderly widows, and dependent survivors of covered male workers were moved from general public relief into the Social Security system, leaving single mothers and the non-white poor to dominate what would come to be called 'welfare'" (Foner, 1999, p. 328). The bifurcation between "social security" and "welfare" has continued to the present day, with the former politically popular and the latter racially charged and negatively perceived (Delaney & Edwards-Levy, 2018, February 5; Skocpol, 1988, p. 302).

While systematic discrimination in the New Deal and afterwards was substantial, the economic roots of the plural society in the South were changing. A major driver was agricultural mechanization, especially for all stages of cotton production. Mechanization in turn hastened out-migration of both black and white agricultural workers. The South became more urbanized, and the planter class began to lose its political control (Quagdano, 1988, p. 254).[8]

Applying the Rule of Law to Dismantle the Legal Framework of America's Divided Society

World War II was a turning point in the attack on America's divided society. There was great industrial demand for labor of black Americans, and this helped spur further emigration from the South (Tolnay, 2003). The migration of millions of black people gave them political power in the North to an extent they had never had before (Klarman, 1994, February, pp. 30–31). Wartime labor shortages meant that black people obtained job opportunities that had been foreclosed to them (Klarman, 1994, February, p. 20). Also, the purpose of the European war itself, to fight extreme racism in Nazi Germany, encouraged overcoming some U.S. practices of discrimination and segregation. Thus, a concurring judge in the 1948 California case of *Perez v. Sharp*, invalidating a ban on interracial marriage, argued:

> Let us not forget that [Hitler] was the man who plunged the world into a war in which, for the third time, Americans fought, bled, and died for the truth of the proposition that all men are created equal. We may take judicial notice of the fact – since it is a political and historical fact – that steady inroads have been made on the myth of racial superiority and its outgrowths. . . . In my opinion, the statutes here involved violate the very premise on which this country and its Constitution were built, the very ideas embodied in the Declaration of Independence, the very issue over which the Revolutionary War, the Civil War, and the Second World War were fought, and the spirit in which the Constitution must be interpreted.
>
> (32 Cal.2d 711 [L.A. No. 20305. In Bank. Oct. 1, 1948], concurring opinion of Carter, J.)

The Cold War also played a part, as U.S. leaders sought to avoid becoming discredited in the global contest to persuade people of the value of the American system of democracy (Klinker & Smith, 1999, p. 249). Finally, federal spending in the South for growing national defense and domestic programs, especially after World War II, lessened dominance of the planter elite and created a constituency of southern businesspeople who sought to accommodate desegregation rather than fight it (Klarman, 1994, February, p. 47).

Actions to overcome constraints of the divided society came from President Harry S. Truman, who issued executive orders barring racial segregation of the armed forces,[9] prohibiting discriminatory personnel actions by federal civilian agencies,[10] and improving practices of other organizations doing business with the federal government.[11] While Truman was personally sensitive to the harm that racial discrimination could cause, he appears to have issued his executive order on desegregating the military in response to skillful lobbying by A. Phillip Randolph and other black leaders (Klinker & Smith, 1999, pp. 217–221).

The courts too were active in attacking race discrimination. Decisions included *Morgan v. Virginia* (1946), declaring unconstitutional "an act of Virginia, which requires all passenger motor vehicle carriers, both interstate and intrastate, to separate without discrimination the white and colored passengers in their motor buses so that contiguous seats will not be occupied by persons of different races at the same time"; *Shelley v. Kramer* (1948), holding that, under the Fourteenth Amendment, state courts could not enforce racially restrictive covenants that exclude "persons of designated race or color from the ownership or occupancy of real property"; and the landmark case of *Brown v. Board of Education of Topeka Kansas* (1954),[12] overturning *Plessy v. Ferguson* (1896) and holding that "in the field of public education the doctrine of 'separate but equal' has no place. Separate educational facilities are inherently unequal." In 1957 President Dwight Eisenhower called in federal troops to enforce court-ordered desegregation of Central High School in Little Rock, overcoming the opposition of Arkansas Governor Orval Faubus.

Once again, the reaction of states, especially in the South, was massive noncompliance. Professor Michael Klarman contends that *Brown* increased the intransigence of southerners against integration. He argues that, rather than directly desegregating southern schools, *Brown* led to entrenched resistance (Klarman, 1994, February, p. 76). Martin Luther King, Jr. and the Civil Rights Movement needed to devise a new strategy to address southern intransigence:

> King and his colleagues had basically given up on convincing southern whites of the wrongness of racial segregation and had redirected their energies toward converting northern whites to the civil rights cause by exposing the true evils of the Jim Crow system. . . . The success of [the new] strategy required not only that the demonstrators remain generally nonviolent and that their objectives be widely perceived as legitimate but also that such political figures as Bull Connor in Birmingham and Jim Clark in Selma "cooperate" by so brutalizing peaceful demonstrators so as to mobilize national opinion behind a legislative assault on Jim Crow.
>
> (Klarman, 1994, February, pp. 141, 143–144)[13]

Only after the events of Birmingham and Selma were Presidents Kennedy and Johnson able to muster the legislative support needed to enact the Civil Rights Act of 1964 and the Voting Rights Act of 1965.[14] The Civil Rights Act of 1964 provided, among other provisions, that, "All persons shall be entitled to the full and equal enjoyment of the goods, services, facilities, and privileges, advantages, and accommodations of any place of public accommodation . . . without discrimination or segregation on the ground of race, color, religion, or national origin," and prohibited employment discrimination against "any individual because of his race, color, religion, sex, or national origin." The Voting Rights Act of 1965, besides establishing the right to vote guaranteed by the Fourteenth and Fifteenth Amendments to the Constitution and undoing many discriminatory laws and practices that southern states adopted after the Civil War, also provided for effective enforcement. Together these two pieces of legislation "stand as impressive achievements, extending political and civil rights to black Americans and eradicating the legal basis for much of the racial hierarchy that had characterized American life for nearly 100 years" (Klinker & Smith, 1999, p. 278).

From the perspective of the divided society as a colonial vestige, it is noteworthy that Dr. King's strategy built on the success of Mahatma Gandhi in helping to break British rule over India. As Dr. King wrote:

> As I delved deeper into the philosophy of Gandhi my skepticism concerning the power of love gradually diminished, and I came to see for the first time its potency in the area of social reform. . . . [I]n the nonviolent resistance philosophy of Gandhi . . . I came to feel that this was the only morally and practically sound method open to oppressed people in their struggle for freedom.
>
> (King, 1958, pp. 96–97)

The lesson of the Civil Rights Movement, and of Mahatma Gandhi before, is that well-designed appeals to legitimacy can be superior in many ways to attempts at using force to overcome constraints of the divided society. It took the Civil Rights Movement, and tactics borrowed from Gandhi's success, to convince large American majorities of the illegitimacy of maintaining a divided society. Backed by a strong constituency, the rule of law could expand through court decisions, presidential leadership, and new legislation to disestablish the legal framework of the divided society.

A high point of the Civil Rights Movement came with the presidency of Lyndon Johnson. In only a few short years, President Johnson moved the Congress to enact not only the Civil Rights Act of 1964 and the Voting Rights Act of 1965 but also major pieces of legislation in a "Great Society" program designed to address widespread poverty that still existed in the United States, and especially in the black community: the Economic

Opportunity Act of 1964, the Food Stamp Act of 1964, the Elementary and Secondary Education Act in 1965, and the Social Security Act of 1965, which created Medicare and Medicaid. In all of these actions, the President was acutely aware of the need to translate good intentions into practical reality. His address at Howard University in 1966, "To Fulfill These Rights," focused almost entirely on that issue:

> It was 100 years ago that a civil war was fought in this country to free the Negro from slavery. The Negro won that war, but he lost the battle still to come. Emancipation was a proclamation, but it was not a fact. I came here tonight to tell you that in the time allotted me, with whatever energy and ability I have, I do not intend for history to repeat itself.
>
> True, more legislation has been signed in the last few months and few years; true, Negro opportunity has been proclaimed. But we must go on to make it a fact.
>
> (Johnson, 1966)

While major programs of the Great Society provided benefits over subsequent decades, others, especially to the extent that they evolved to become programs supporting excessive incarceration of people from African American low-income neighborhoods, had negative effects (e.g., Alexander, 2012, pp. 45–47). Another significant piece of legislation, enacted in the last year of Lyndon Johnson's presidency, was the Fair Housing Act of 1968, which prohibited discrimination in the sale, rental, and financing of housing based on race, religion, or national origin. However, both poor implementation of the act and the limited remedies that authorities sought under the act meant that its effects were more modest than they might have been (Krysan & Crowder, 2017, p. 9). Now that the legal framework of the divided society has been largely dismantled, with legal cases continuing to explore its bounds, currently in voting rights and affirmative action in education, the focus of many has shifted to overcoming the patterns of behavior that the legal framework has shaped.

Notes

1. Scholars have struggled to reconcile the liberal philosophical writings of John Locke with his activities supporting the slave trade, including owning

shares in the Royal African Company. See Hinshelwood (2013); Farr (2008); and Glausser (1990).

2. For example, the exchange between John Rutledge of South Carolina and Roger Sherman of Connecticut during the Constitutional Convention: "Mr. Sherman said it was better to let the Southern States import slaves than to part with them if they made that a *sine qua non*" (Scott, 1893, pp. 582–583).
3. Payment to slave owners but lack of compensation to slaves themselves represents a pattern of resolving issues by paying off politically powerful actors while leaving more deserving but politically weak stakeholders to fend for themselves. The United States recently underwent such an experience when government bailed out large banks in the financial crisis while largely neglecting claims of homeowners whom the banks had harmed by selling subprime and other unsustainable mortgage products. This occurred even though economists contend that it would have been far more effective to assist over-indebted homeowners than to bail out financial firms that had extended homeowners too much credit (Mian & Sufi, 2015).
4. The long effort to outlaw slavery and the aftermath of abolition of the slave trade and emancipation are recounted well in Morgan (2007, pp. 148–171). With respect to South Asians in the plural society of Caribbean colonies, see Smith (1965, p. 7) ("In Trinidad and British Guiana, where Indian immigration continued for decades on a substantial scale, the immigrants were concentrated on plantations in conditions which ensured social and ethnic isolation") and Tinker (1974).
5. It was the southern elite who owned slaves: "Slaveholding was reserved for the top echelon of white households, with an even smaller minority owning a large plantation. In 1860, 21 percent of white southern households owned at least one slave and 0.5 percent owned 50 or more slaves" (Ager, Boustan, & Eriksson, 2019, March, p. 5, citation omitted).
6. "Defining vagrancy in sweeping terms, these nine [southern] states gave local authorities a virtual mandate to arrest any poor man who did not have a labor contract" (Cohen, 1976, p. 47).
7. To this list of cases enshrining the divided society, Professor Richard Pildes would add *Giles v. Harris*, 189 U.S. 475 (1903), upholding nominally neutral state constitutional provisions that limited voting rights. See Pildes (2000).
8. Quagdano (1988, p. 254): "Thus, even before the civil rights movement transformed the political structure of the South, the proportion of southern blacks registered to vote had increased from 5 percent in 1940 to 28 percent in 1960."
9. Executive Order 9981 – "Establishing the President's Committee on Equality of Treatment and Opportunity in the Armed Services," July 26, 1948 ("It is hereby declared to be the policy of the President that there shall be equality of treatment and opportunity for all persons in the armed services without regard to race, color, religion or national origin. This policy shall be put into effect as rapidly as possible, having due regard to the time required to effectuate any necessary changes without impairing efficiency or morale").

10. Executive Order 9980 – "Regulations Governing Fair Employment Practices Within the Federal Establishment," July 26, 1948 ("All personnel actions taken by Federal appointing officers shall be based solely on merit and fitness; and such officers are authorized and directed to take appropriate steps to insure that in all such actions there shall be no discrimination because of race, color, religion, or national origin").
11. For example, Executive Order 10308 – "Improving the Means for Obtaining Compliance with the Nondiscrimination Provisions of Federal Contracts," December 3, 1951.
12. Decided May 17, 1954.
13. The term "Jim Crow laws" applied to strict segregation laws enacted in the South after the Civil War. C. Vann Woodward (1966, p. 7) notes that the origin of the term is not known.
14. See Lichtman (1969, p. 365, footnote omitted):

    Savage suppression of the Selma demonstrations once again compelled the realization among Congress and the public that new measures were needed. A new voting rights bill was drafted in the Civil Rights Division and presented to Congress in March, 1965. This bill, which became law that Summer, provided for the use of federal registration examiners and election observers in localities applying discriminatory registration standards or refusing to provide adequate access to registration or voting.

Sources Cited

Ager, P., Boustan, L. P., & Eriksson, K. (2019, March). The intergenerational effects of a large wealth shock: White southerners after the civil war. NBER Working Paper, Cambridge, MA.

Alexander, A. (2012). *The new Jim Crow: Mass incarceration in the age of colorblindness* (Rev. ed.). New York, NY: The New Press.

Ash, S. V. (1991). Poor whites in the occupied South, 1861–1865. *The Journal of Southern History*, *57*(1), 39–62.

Beckert, S. (2015). *Empire of cotton: A global history*. New York, NY: Alfred A. Knopf.

Blackmon, D. (2009). *Slavery by another name: The re-enslavement of Black Americans from the civil war to world war II*. New York, NY: Anchor Books.

Cohen, W. (1976). Negro involuntary servitude in the South, 1865–1940: A preliminary analysis. *The Journal of Southern History*, *42*(1), 31–60.

Degler, C. N. (1959). Slavery and the genesis of American race prejudice. *Comparative Studies in Society and History*, *2*(1), 49–66.

Delaney, A., & Edwards-Levy, A. (2018, February 5). Americans are mistaken about who gets welfare: People significantly overestimate the number of African-Americans benefiting from the largest programs. *Huffington Post*. Retrieved from www.huffingtonpost.com/entry/americans-welfare-perceptions-survey_us_5a7880cde4b0d3df1d13f60b

Drescher, S. (1994). Whose abolition? Popular pressure and the ending of the British slave trade. *Past and Present*, *143*(136–166).

Farr, J. (2008). Locke, natural law, and new world slavery. *Political Theory, 36*(4), 495–522.

Finegold, K. (1988). Agriculture and the politics of U.S. social provision: Social insurance and food stamps. In M. Weir, A. S. Orloff, & T. Skocpol (Eds.), *The politics of social policy in the United States*. Princeton, NJ: Princeton University Press.

Finkelman, P. (1987). Slavery and the constitutional convention: Making a covenant with death. In R. Beeman, S. Botein, & E. C. C. II (Eds.), *Beyond confederation: Origins of the constitution and American national identity* (pp. 188–225). Chapel Hill, NC: Institute of Early American History and Culture, University of North Carolina Press.

Finkelman, P. (2002). The proslavery origins of the electoral college. *Cardozo Law Review, 23*(4), 1145–1157.

Foner, E. (1988). *Reconstruction: America's unfinished revolution, 1863–1877*. New York, NY: Harper and Row.

Foner, E. (1999). Expert report of Eric Foner. *Michigan Journal of Race and Law, 5*, 311–338.

Glausser, W. (1990, April-June). Three approaches to Locke and the slave trade. *Journal of the History of Ideas, 51*(2), 199–216.

Higginbotham, A. L., Jr. (1978). *In the matter of color: Race and the American legal process, the colonial period*. New York, NY: Oxford University Press.

Hinshelwood, B. (2013). The Carolinian context of John Locke's theory of slavery. *Political Theory, 41*(4), 562–590.

Holden, M., Jr. (1996). Public administration and the plural society. In *Continuity and disruption: Essays in public administration*. Pittsburgh, PA: University of Pittsburgh Press.

Hurd, J. C. (1858). *The law of freedom and bondage* (Vol. 1). Boston, MA: Little, Brown, and Company.

Huttenback, R. A. (1973). The British empire as a "white man's country": Racial attitudes and immigration legislation in the colonies of white settlement. *Journal of British Studies, 13*(1), 108–137.

Jackson, K. T. (1980). Race, ethnicity, and real estate appraisal: The home owners loan corporation and the federal housing administration. *Journal of Urban History, 6*(4), 419–452.

Johnson, L. B. (1966, June 1–2). *To fulfill these rights*. White House Conference: Speeches.

King, M. L., Jr. (1958). *Stride toward freedom: The Montgomery story*. New York, NY: Harper and Row.

Klarman, M. J. (1994, February). Brown, racial change, and the civil rights movement. *Virginia Law Review, 80*(1), 7–150.

Klinker, P. A., & Smith, R. W. (1999). *The unsteady march: The rise and decline of racial equality in America*. Chicago, IL: University of Chicago Press.

Krysan, M., and Crowder, K. (2017). *Cycle of segregation: social processes and residential stratification*. New York: Russell Sage Foundation.

Lacroix, A. L. (2010). The authority for federalism: Madison's negative and the origins of federal ideology. *Law and History Review*, *28*(2), 451–505.

Lichtman, A. (1969). The federal assault against voting discrimination in the deep South 1957–1967. *The Journal of Negro History*, *54*(4), 346–367.

McCord, D. J. (1840). *Containing the acts relating to Charleston, courts, slaves, and rivers* (Vol. III). Columbia, SC: A. S. Johnston.

Mian, A., & Sufi, A. (2015). *House of debt: How they (and you) caused the great recession and how we can prevent it from happening again*. Chicago, IL: University of Chicago Press.

Morgan, K. (2007). *Slavery and the British empire: From Africa to America*. New York, NY: Oxford University Press.

Morris, R. B. (1954). The measure of bondage in the slave states. *The Mississippi Valley Historical Review*, *41*(2), 219–240.

Myles, J. (1988). Postwar capitalism and the extension of social security into a retirement wage. In M. Weir, A. S. Orloff, & T. Skocpol (Eds.), *The politics of social policy in the United States*. Princeton, NJ: Princeton University Press.

Olwell, R. (1998). *Masters, slaves, and subjects: The culture of power in the South Carolina low country 1740–1790*. Ithaca, NY: Cornell University Press.

Pildes, R. H. (2000). Democracy, anti-democracy, and the cannon. *Constitutional Commentary*, *17*, 295–319.

Quagdano, J. (1988). From old-age assistance to supplemental security income: The political economy of relief in the South, 1935–1972. In M. Weir, A. S. Orloff, & T. Skocpol (Eds.), *The politics of social policy in the United States*. Princeton, NJ: Princeton University Press.

Roberts, C. K. (2012). *The new deal, rural poverty, and the South*. Doctoral dissertation, University of Alabama.

Russell, C. W. (1907, October 10). Report of Hon. Charles W. Russell, Assistant Attorney General, relative to peonage matters. Exhibit 17 to U.S. Attorney General Annual Report.

Scott, E. H. (ed.). (1893). *Journal of the federal convention kept by James Madison*. Chicago, IL: Albert, Scott and Co.

Skocpol, T. (1988). The limits of the new deal system and the roots of contemporary welfare dilemmas. In M. Weir, A. S. Orloff, & T. Skocpol (Eds.), *The politics of social policy in the United States*. Princeton, NJ: Princeton University Press.

Smith, M. G. (1965). *The plural society in the British West Indies*. Berkeley, CA: University of California Press.

Tinker, H. (1974). *A new system of slavery: The export of Indian labour overseas 1830–1920*. London: Oxford University Press.

Tolnay, S. E. (2003). The African American "great migration" and beyond. *Annual Review of Sociology*, *29*, 209–232.

Tolnay, S. E., & Beck, E. M. (1990). Black flight: Lethal violence and the great migration, 1900–1930. *Social Science History*, *14*(3), 347–370.

U.S. National Commission on Urban Problems. (1969). *Building the American city: Report of the national commission on urban problems to the congress and to the president of the United States*. Washington, DC: U.S. Government Printing Office.

Vishneski, J. (1988). What the court decided in Dred Scott v. Sandford. *The American Journal of Legal History*, *32*(4), 373–390.

Wiecek, W. M. (1977a). The statutory law of slavery and race in the thirteen mainland colonies of British America. *The William and Mary Quarterly*, *34*(2), 258–280.

Wiecek, W. M. (1977b). *The sources of anti-slavery constitutionalism in America, 1760–1848*. Ithaca, NY: Cornell University Press.

Wolgemuth, K. L. (1958, November). Woodrow Wilson's appointment policy and the Negro. *The Journal of Southern History*, *24*(4), 457–471.

Wolgemuth, K. L. (1959, April). Woodrow Wilson and federal segregation. *The Journal of Negro History*, *44*(2), 158–173.

Woodward, C. V. (1966). *The strange career of Jim Crow* (2nd ed.). New York, NY: Oxford University Press.

Zeichner, O. (1940). The legal status of the agricultural laborer in the South. *Political Science Quarterly*, *55*(3), 412–428.

Cases Cited

Brown v. Board of Education of Topeka Kansas, 347 U.S. 483, 74 S. Ct. 686, 98 L. Ed. 873 (1954).

Civil Rights Cases, 109 U.S. 3 (1883).

Dred Scott v. Sandford, 60 U.S. 393 (1857).

Giles v. Harris, 189 U.S. 475 (1903).

Hobbs v. Fogg, 6 Watts 553, 1837 WL 3128 (1837, July 1).

Marbury v. Madison, 5 U.S. 137 (1803).

Morgan v. Virginia, 328 U.S. 373, 66 S. Ct. 1050, 90 L. Ed. 1317 (1946).

Perez v. Sharp, 32 Cal.2d 711 (California Supreme Court 1948).

Plessy v. Ferguson, 163 U.S. 537 (1896).

Shelley v. Kramer, 334 US 1, 68 S. Ct. 836, 92 L. Ed. 1161 (1948).

Slaughterhouse Cases, 16 Wallace 36 (1873).

Sommerset v. Stewart, 98 ER 499 (1772).

The State v. John Mann, 13 N.C. 263 (1829).

United States v. Cruikshank, 92 U.S. 542 (U.S. Supreme Court 1876).

United States v. Reese, 92 U.S. 214 (1876).

Williams v. Mississippi, 170 U.S. 213 (U.S. Supreme Court 1898).

Laws and Executive Orders Cited

Civil Rights Act of 1964.

Economic Opportunity Act of 1964.
Elementary and Secondary Education Act of 1965.
Exec. Order No. 9980 (1948).
Exec. Order No. 9981 (1948).
Exec. Order No. 10308 (1951).
Food Stamp Act of 1964.
Fugitive Slave Act of 1850, Lillian Goldman Law Library, The Avalon Project, Yale University Law School, 9 stat. 446 Stat. (1850).
The Fundamental Constitutions of Carolina. Lillian Goldman Law Library, The Avalon Project, and Yale University Law School. (1669, March 1).
Laws of Virginia. (1705, October). *An act concerning servants and slaves.* Retrieved from http://vagenweb.org/hening/vol03-25.htm
Mississippi Vagrant Law. Retrieved from http://web.mit.edu/21h.102/www/Primary%20source%20collections/Reconstruction/Black%20codes.htm (1865).
Social Security Act of 1965.
Voting Rights Act of 1965.

5 Conclusion

Overcoming the Colonial History of America's Divided Society

Even with the legal framework of the divided society largely disestablished, the legacy of the colonial divided society continues to influence America's society and economy. A salient effect of earlier legal barriers has their contribution to a continuing division of races according to the neighborhoods where many people reside (Glaeser & Vigdor, 2012). While many black Americans today have risen into the middle and upper classes and are increasingly included in the American political elite, many others still find themselves in the bottom ranks of economic success, often concentrated in distinct neighborhoods of urban areas (e.g., Alexander, 2012, pp. 195–196). The separation of races and income classes by neighborhood leads to further social division, such as racially unbalanced primary and secondary schools.

Besides reflecting continuation of the divided society, living in racially separate neighborhoods can have serious consequences for the affected people. In addition to other needed responses, civic networks can play important roles in helping to overcome a divided society. This is more than a tautology. The civic networks to which people belong are important to help them to obtain mentorship and other guidance about work and education, and to offer the personal introductions that can affect a person's mobility in society. In the United States, civic networks tend to be stratified. A McKinsey study concludes that:

> [E]conomic, social, cultural, and political networks and institutions . . . tend to reinforce existing socioeconomic patterns. For instance, communities with high levels of economic activity and rich social networks tend to produce more affluent families and contain assets (such as homes and businesses) that are valued more

> highly. Conversely, communities that lack economic activity and connections to opportunities tend to perform poorly.
>
> (Noel, Pinder, Stewart, & Wright, 2019, p. 9)

Residential separation, and other sources of the divide in the civic networks to which people belong, then create feedback loops that can reinforce social divisions among races:

> [T]he separation of different racial and ethnic groups into distinct and qualitatively different residential spaces produces sharp racial differences in sociodemographic characteristics and life experiences that, in turn, shape profound racial differences in residential search processes and neighborhood outcomes. The resulting racial stratification in patterns of residential mobility and immobility continually perpetuates residential stratification into subsequent generations and across time, even in the absence of overt efforts to maintain the residential color line.
>
> (Krysan & Crowder, 2017, p. 11)

These dynamics promote social and economic stratification even when legal barriers have been removed. From the perspective of America's colonial history, perhaps the most serious vestige of the colonial experience is the way that a divided society continues to hinder the ability of interracial civic networks to form (see Noel et al., 2019; Chetty, Hendren, Jones, & Porter, 2019).

Thus, while there has been substantial long-term progress, much remains to be done. The colonial and post-colonial laws that structured and preserved the divided society in the United States have had long-term effects because of the way that they impeded the development of positive interracial relationships and the civic networks that can help to promote a stronger society.[1] It is especially difficult to form such networks when differences in both race and economic status must be bridged at the same time. On the other hand, the Anglo-American tradition of the rule of law, also a colonial legacy, has supported clear, if uneven, progress in the United States to overcome the social division that has persisted for so many years.

Many in the United States continue to seek a more unified society: to continue the process of building the cross-racial civic networks that are the antithesis of a divided society. And the rule of law continues to play a role, creating a large and growing body of law that underscores the legitimacy of efforts to overcome the racially divided society so that the United States finally becomes a fully post-colonial nation.

Note

1. The McKinsey researchers point also (Noel et al., 2019, pp. 5–6) to the substantial increased economic benefits to the entire society and economy of the United States that can result from building more integrated civic networks.

Sources Cited

Alexander, A. (2012). *The new Jim Crow: Mass incarceration in the age of colorblindness* (Rev. ed.). New York, NY: The New Press.

Chetty, R., Hendren, N., Jones, M. R., & Porter, S. R. (2019, June). Race and economic opportunity in the United States: An intergenerational perspective. NBER Working Paper No. 24441.

Glaeser, E., & Vigdor, J. (January, 2012). The end of the segregated century: Racial separation in America's neighborhoods, 1890–2010. Report, Manhattan Institute.

Krysan, M., & Crowder, K. (2017). *Cycle of segregation: Social processes and residential stratification*. New York, NY: Russell Sage Foundation.

Noel, N., Pinder, D., Stewart, S., & Wright, J. (2019, August). *The economic impact of closing the racial wealth gap*. New York, NY: McKinsey and Company.

Index

13 American colonies; 16, 20, 22; divided societies and 9–20; economic drivers of British colonialism and 5, 6; and other settler colonies (list of) 5; slavery laws and 2, 35

Abolition (*also* Abolitionist) 8, 40–42, 55
American Revolution (*also* Revolutionary War) 7, 16, 18–20, 22, 38, 51

Barrow, T. C. 6
Beckert, Sven 41; *The Empire of Cotton* 17
Beer, George Louis 5
Bickel, Alexander 27
Black Codes 44–45
Board of Trade 6
Boston Tea Party 6
Brazil, race discrimination 29–30
British colonial economies 1; 13 American colonies and 2, 5, 6; American colonies in a position of economic subordination 6; contribution to racial, ethnic, and religious strife 4; cotton 7–8, 10; East India Company 5, 6; Hudson's Bay Company 5; indigo 7, 10; investors 4, 5, 6, 8; joint-stock companies 4–5, 7; mercantilist philosophy 6; neocolonialism 8; rice 7; Royal African Company 1; royal companies 6; Russia Company 5; slave trade 7–8; sugar 7, 9–10, 40, 41; tea 6; Tea Party (1773) 6; tobacco 6, 7; unwillingness to pay for administration 6–7; West Indies 7
British Empire 4, 8, 11, 16, 17, 20, 39–41
Burma 9, 10, 12; *see also*, Myanmar

Caribbean colonies 5, 9, 12, 41
Chanock, Martin 21
Citizenship 10, 25, 28, 42, 45
Civic network 61–62
Civil Rights Act of 1964 52–53
colonial rule 1
colonization: for economic gain 4, 5, 8; as remedy for overpopulation 5
Companies Acts 5
Cottrol, Robert 30–31
Crown Colony 11

Declaration of Independence 6, 23, 51
Degler, Carl 29
Dicey, Albert Venn 19, 24
divided societies (*also* plural societies) 9–13; 13 American colonies as 9–10; Asian laborers (imported) 12; British Empire 9; Caribbean colonies 12; cash crops and slavery 9–10; Chinese in 12; colonialism 12; divided societies after colonial ruler

departs 11–13; divided society compared to pluralism 10; due to laws 2; Fiji 12; formation of interracial civic networks and 62–63; homogeneous society 10; India 13; indigenous politics 13; indigo 10; Indonesia 12; melting pot 10; mosaic (Canada) 10; Native Americans 12; rice 10, 12; Rohingya 12; rule by law and 2; rule of law 22; rule of law and colonial 19; South Asians 12; sugar 9–10; United States 12; *see also* J.S. Furnivall (plural society) 9–13; *see also* rule of law to dismantle America's divided society; *see also* United States as divided society
Dyer, General R. E. H. 24

economic drivers: of American slavery 7, 8; of British colonialism 4–9
Economist, The 12
Eisenhower, Dwight 52
Emancipation 40–41, 54, 55

Fair Housing Act of 1968 54
Federal Housing Administration (FHA) 48–49
Ferguson, Niall 7
Field, Stephen 45–46
Fiji 12
Finkelman, Paul 39
Foner, Eric 47
Fraenkel, Ernst 23–24; *The Dual State: A Contribution to the Theory of Dictatorship* 23
Friedman, Barry 26
Friedman, Lawrence 25–27
Furnivall, J. S. 9, 10, 12, 13, 29, 49; *Colonial Policy and Practice* 9; *see also* Plural Societies

Gandhi, Mahatma 53
Georgia 7, 36
Greene, Jack 6

Hastings, Warren 16
Hawkins, John 7
Higginbotham, Leon, Jr. 36, 39
Holden, Matthew 29, 43
Holmes, Stephen 28
Home Owners Loan Corporation (HOLC) 48
Hussain, Nasser 24

India 5, 11, 13, 41, 53

Johnson, Lyndon 52, 53–54
Judicial review 26–27

King, Martin Luther, Jr. 52, 53
Klarman, Michael 52

Latin America, discrimination 29–30
Legitimacy 1, 19–20, 27, 28, 53, 63
Lincoln, Abraham 42
Locke, John 35

Malaysia (formerly British Malaya) 12
Massachusetts 36
Merivale, Herman 40
Mississippi Vagrant Law 44
Morgan, Kenneth 35, 40
Mukherjee, Mithi: *India in the Shadows of Empire: A Legal and Political History 1774–1950* 16
Munn, Christopher 18
Myanmar 12; *see also* Burma

National Socialism 23
Native Americans 12
Navigation Acts 6
New York 36
North Carolina 37

Pennsylvania 36
pluralism compared to plural society 10
plural societies *see* divided societies
Pollock, Frederick: "The History of English Law as a Branch of Politics" 20
post-colonial authoritarian rule 13

Randolph, A. Phillip 51
Raz, Joseph 22

Reconstruction (post-Civil War) 28–29, 45
Revolutionary War (*see* American Revolution)
Rhode Island 8
Roosevelt, Franklin 26, 47, 49
rule by law: administration of 29; Amritsar massacre of 1919 (Jallianwala Bagh massacre) 24, 25; anti-Chinese statutes 18; black Americans in early 20th century 47; British colonies and 16, 18; difference from rule of law 19–20; dual legal system 23; dual state 23–24; East India Company 16; emancipated slaves and 2; enslaved people 2, 39–40; Germany under National Socialist rule 23; Hong Kong 18; India 16, 18, 24; law as an instrument of control 17; legitimacy and 27; martial law 24; race-based laws 17; racism 18; racism in Nazi Germany 50; and post-Civil War Reconstruction 29; slavery and law 35–43; state of emergency 24, 25; terms of the slaveowner relationship in law 35, 36; white supremacy and 17–18.
rule of law: 13 American colonies and 16, 17, 18, 20, 22; American Revolution 18–19, 22; in British colonies 16–19; British legacy to United States 1–3; citizenship laws 25; colonial divided society and 19; contradiction in how the British ruled India 16; Declaration of Independence 23; Dicey's 19, 24; difference from rule by law 19–20; differing meanings of 21–25; divided society and 22; *Dred Scott v. Sandford* 19; English Bill of Rights 19; form of government in a rule-of-law system 19; ; importance of 20–21; overcoming social division in the U.S. 62; property rights 19; rule of law (term) 20–21; rule of law and attributes of a democratic society 22; segregation and 50–51; significance of 16–31; *Sommerset v. Stewart* 19; United States Constitution and 19, 25–32;
rule of law to dismantle America's divided society 2, 50–54; *Brown v. Board of Education of Topeka Kansas* 52; Central High School in Little Rock 52; Civil Rights Act of 1964 52–53; Civil Rights Movement 52–53; desegregation 51; Fair Housing Act of 1968 54; Fifteenth Amendment 53; Fourteenth Amendment 53; *Morgan v. Virginia* 51; *Perez v. Sharp* 51; *Plessy v. Ferguson* 52; *Shelley v. Kramer* 52; Voting Rights Act of 1965 52–53

Scott, William Robert 7
settler colonies 5
sharecropping 45, 47, 49
Shklar, Judith 24
slavery 2, 4, 7–9, 20–25, 35–42, 47, 54, 55
Smith, M. G. 13
Smith, Peter-Wesley 18
Smith, Rogers: *Civic Ideals: Conflicting Visions of Citizenship in U.S. History* 25
South Africa 5, 17
South Carolina 7, 35, 36, 37
Sri Lanka (formerly the colony of Ceylon) 12
stratified American colonial society 1; *see* divided societies
sugar cane 9

Tamanaha, Brian 21–22
Thompson, E. P. 20–21
Three-fifths Compromise (*see* United States Constitution)
Tocqueville, Alexis de 10–11
trade (goods) 4, 6–7, 8, 17, 40, 41
Trinidad (colony) 11
Trinidad and Tobago (post-colonial) 11
Truman, Harry S. 51
Tyler, Tom R. 19

United States as divided society 43–50; abolishing slavery 38, 42, 43; American divided society 37–38; anti-peonage law 46; Applying the Rule of Law to Dismantle the Legal Framework of America's Divided Society 50–56; Articles of Confederation and interests of slaves states 38–39; the Black Codes 31n2, 44–45; Britain abolishing slavery and 39, 40–41; British Caribbean colonies 41; Chinese 48; *Civil Rights Cases* 46; Constitution 41; cotton industry 41, 43, 47, 49, 50; *Dred Scott v. Sandford* 42; electoral college 39; emancipation of slaves and law in 38, 40–41, 43, 45, 47; enslaved people as property in law 36–37; equal, but separate 46–47; Federal Housing Administration (FHA) racial discrimination against blacks 48–49; Fifteenth Amendment 43; Fourteenth Amendment 39, 42, 45; Fugitive Slave Act (1850) 42; Great Depression relief programs 47, 48, 49; Home Owners Loan Corporation (HOLC) 48; killing enslaved people not considered a felony 36; legal restrictions on blacks post-Civil War 43–50; Mississippi Vagrant Law 44; New Deal and systemic discrimination 2, 49, 50; Old Age Insurance 50; overcoming colonial history 61–63; *Plessy v. Ferguson* 46–47; race riots 47–48; red lining practice 48;lack of redress by enslaved people 37; segregation 47; *Slaughterhouse Cases* 45–46; slavery and law 35–43; Social Security Act of 1935 49–50; social security and welfare 50; *Sommerset v. Stewart* 39; South Asians 48; *The State v. John Mann* 37; systemic race-based discrimination 12; terms of the slaveowner relationship in law 35, 36; thirteen British North American colonies 35; Thirteenth Amendment 42; *United States v. Cruikshank* 46; *United States v. Reese* 46; Veterans Administration (VA) 48; West Indian sugar 40; *Williams v. Mississippi* 46

United States Constitution: Constitutional compromises 38–39; and rule by law 2; and rule of law 25–32; slavery laws and 2; slave trade and 39

United States Constitution and the rule of law: compared to antidiscrimination laws in Latin America 29, 30; Bill of Rights 25; *Brown v. Board of Education* 27–28; dismantling barriers of divided societies 28; compared to divided societies and other former colonies 28; divided society in America from a public administration point of view 29; Fourteenth Amendment 27, 39, 42, 45, 53; legitimacy and rule of law 27; *Marbury v. Madison* 26; New Deal legislation 26; compared to race-based discrimination in Brazil 30; Reconstruction 29; rule of law as stable fixture of American governance 27; slave trade 39; U.S. judicial review process 26–27

Virginia 36, 51–52

Weber, Max 23

Williams, Eric 11; *see also* Trinidad and Tobago

Wilson, Woodrow 47

Woodward, C. Vann 29